THE TRUTH ABOUT SUCCESS

MEGGAN LARSON

Foreword by MARTHA KREJCI

with LAUREN DA SILVA

with NATASHA LOOHUYS

with CHRISTIANNA JOHNSON

with DAWN SHANNON

with ROSILAH SANI

with NATALIE RODRIGUEZ

with JENNA HERRIG

with TOBI B FELDMAN

with CYNTHIA MAE

with ANGELA NEWHOUSE

with DEBBIE ROTHE

with RACHEL KUEHN

with GRETA OLECHNO

with LYNN EADS

with ANNA STAGER

with LA SHEONDA SANCHEZ

with KOREEN CHANDLER

with JILL COLETTI

with RACHEL TIBOLD

with JO PRONGER FAULKNER

with MEGAN DALE

with DEBBIE DEAN

with CAROLYNN SAUER

with FAYE HARTZELL

FLY WITH ME PUBLISHING

Copyright © 2021 Fly With Me Publishing

Library and Archives Canada Cataloguing in Publications.

Copyright in Ontario Canada.

For permissions contact:

hello@megganlarson.com

E-Book ISBN: 978-1-7774164-6-1

Print ISBN: 978-1-7774164-5-4

1st Edition

CONTENTS

FOREWORD

It's a very rare experience these days to find humans so pure of heart that they reach out into the world to lift others up.

I say it's rare NOW....however, with books like this, that won't be long. Stories of success and triumph in the face of fear and obstacles is what we all need, in my opinion, and the more we dig into calling out each other's wins, the more we move away from the current state of the world and into a world that loves and supports each other regardless of personal gain.

I'm beyond proud of Meggan and the beautiful ladies that shared their stories in this book.

The future is being modelled to you right now.

This is how we shift the whole planet.

Let's GOOO!!!!

Xo Martha

Martha Krejci, Business Growth Expert and Founder of Home-Based Revolution (HBR)

I

AUTHENTICITY & INSPIRATION

THE TRUTH ABOUT SUCCESSFULLY STEPPING INTO YOUR AUTHENTIC SELF

MEGGAN LARSON

"She's no one."

The words echoed in my mind as I plastered a smile on my face.

We were out for coffee and her co-worker had come to our table, looked back and forth between us, and bluntly asked who I was (since I looked almost exactly like her). Instead of introducing me, she told the woman that I was no one, and that she'd explain later.

I can still feel the shame bubbling up inside of my chest when I think about that experience. I was fifteen, and she was my biological mother.

From the moment those words were spoken, and because I agreed with them, I spent my life hiding in the shadows. I kept very quiet and didn't make eye contact with people. I believed that I was worthless, so I slept around and kept myself emotionally unavailable. I mimicked others like a chameleon, never understanding that I was struggling with my identity because I was looking to others for validation. Deep down I believed that I was unlovable and that there was something intrinsically wrong with me. If my own parents didn't want me, then what did that say about me?

Any time I considered opening my mouth to share an opinion, I would be overcome with insecurity. *What if what I say offends someone? What if someone takes it the wrong way? What if I hurt someone's feelings?*

I didn't let anyone come close enough to get to know the real me because I figured they would leave the moment they did. I told myself that it was easier that way, safer even. In reality it was lonely, and I was playing the supporting character in my own life instead of the leading role.

I wound up burying the shame I felt about my existence and eventually found Jesus (highly recommend), married the love of my life, and started having kids. On the outside my life seemed pretty good, but inside I longed for more. I knew that I wanted more out of life than what I was living, but I had no idea what that looked like or where to start.

I was then introduced to a business seminar taking place over 2,700 miles away. I was working multiple jobs and still drowning, so I decided to give it a shot. I fell in love with the idea of being an entrepreneur and the thought of becoming a stay-at-home multi-millionaire mom was pretty appealing. The problem was, I still didn't trust people. I knew that if I was going to succeed as an entrepreneur, then I would need to change. I couldn't hope to build trust with people if I didn't like them.

For years I worked on my personal growth while I watched others race ahead of me. I worked hard to overcome the negative mindset that being abandoned by my birth parents had left me with. I struggled through learning how to trust people, believe the best in people, and overcome the many challenges thrown my way including cancer, two babies in critical care at the hospital, and a life-threatening pregnancy.

I did everything I was told to do. I called thousands upon

thousands of leads (and paid for the privilege of being hung up on multiple times a day), read scripts, listened to training so often that I developed callouses in my ears, and repeated it over and over and over again to no avail.

I didn't feel authentic; I felt as though I were manipulating people into a sale, but what did I know? It's what the "experts" were telling me to do, so I did it. It got to the point where the woman who led the business seminars I had been attending for over a decade finally gave me permission to quit. So I did.

During those years, I walked on eggshells around my biological family, hoping they would love and accept me as their own. I made sure never to say or do anything inflammatory, and I stuffed down my feelings, thoughts, and true opinions so I wouldn't jeopardize the relationships. It never occurred to me that they didn't take the same care with my feelings, or that I was also walking on eggshells with everyone else in my life.

More moments like the coffee-shop incident occurred, and I tried to explain them away to myself.

That woman was just a coworker who wasn't aware that my mother had given a child up for adoption. She wasn't about to explain all of that in a Starbucks.

That relative didn't know about me yet.

Surely a funeral wasn't the time or place for an announcement about an illegitimate child.

The truth was, though, that she was never going to accept me as hers and I knew it, so I set my sights on finding my birth father instead. It was easier for me to believe that my worth and validation would be found in others, but instead the conclusion that

I came to was very different than the one I had expected. Though I found my birth father quickly and he was more amazing than I ever could have dreamed, I still felt lost and unfulfilled.

I threw myself into my job because it was easier and safer for me to support the dreams of others instead of chasing my own. I let myself be overworked and underpaid because I believed that it was for the greater good. If I couldn't have my own dreams, surely I could support someone reaching for theirs. I was on the verge of a nervous breakdown and even further away from my identity than ever.

Just when all hope seemed lost, I came across a strategist who was talking about a new way to do business that *served* people instead of manipulating them. I was hooked from day one. She was teaching people how to tune into their authentic selves and serve from their hearts, offering what they were most passionate about. Working with her taught me how to find my identity and true purpose, and to my shock, it wasn't found in anyone else but me.

I started to play with the idea of showing up as myself. I began blogging on my own website instead of simply ghost-writing for others. I changed how I was showing up on social media, and I even started making YouTube videos. I was talking about the things that I was passionate about, and it turns out I had a lot to say.

Then I noticed that the more I stepped out as myself, the harder those around me tried to pull me down. Sadly, this was coming from the very people I'd naively assumed would want me to shine. I was being told to retreat, to stop speaking out, and return to the corner where they felt I belonged. I was at the biggest fork in the road of my life. Faced with the choice between disappointing friends and family or disappointing myself. Historically, I had always chosen to silence my voice for the sake of others, but I knew that I couldn't keep doing the same thing over and over again and expect a different result. This was my moment to step out from behind everyone else's shadow, and it was absolutely terrifying.

What if I fell flat on my face? What if the words that had been spoken to me and about me were true? What if I failed miserably? My business-coach-turned-friend, Martha Krejci, saw something in me that I didn't yet see in myself. She believed in me enough for both of us, and so I leapt off that mountain and instead of falling on my face, I began to fly. People took notice and fell in step with me. People liked what I had to say; it resonated with them, and they wanted more of it. People bought my courses and started paying me to coach them. My husband came home full time so that we could continue to soar together.

I've lost some relationships along the way that I'd never expected to lose, but I've come to realize that those very relationships had kept me just comfortable enough not to show up. The tribe I have now wants me to show up authentically. They cheer me on and challenge me in unexpected ways. Had I not let go of the relationships, thoughts, and beliefs that had kept me stuck for so long, I wouldn't have had room for this new tribe in my life. Sometimes you have to let go of what's comfortable in order to receive what's indescribable.

A dear friend of mine wrote these words recently, and she has given me permission to share them with you here.

"I'm what some personality tests will call a yellow or pearl personality. People with this personality tend to be too caring and giving. Down to our own detriment. And for years I was. Then I wised up, grew a backbone and stopped allowing others to manipulate me. That is the day that my days of lack stopped. You see, some will spot that caring and giving side of you which, when on a mission, will stop at nothing, and they want to use that to their advantage.

"Because when we buckle down, we are money makers, and we also know how to fix what's broken and stop the BS in its tracks. We hold down the fort and are protective to a level that makes a momma bear protecting her cubs look weak. The greatest thing individuals who are pearl or yellow personality can do is learn to discern. Not everyone wants relationships with you even when they say they do. Some just want what you can do for them. And while it's okay to do for others, it's also important to have boundaries.

"Your biggest challenge will always be that red/ ruby personality. They're driven by money, luxury and popularity. While none are bad, it can become destructive if neither you nor that red personality have boundaries. That red personality will pump you up and get you excited about *their* vision. So much that you can forget *your* vision and *your* path. The next thing you know, you don't even recognize who you are or what you're working for.

"For us yellows, that can lead to an ugly spiral of depression and resentment, and we can't blame anyone but ourselves. It's not red's fault. It's ours for being so sold out on our drug of mission and purpose that we didn't stop to analyze." — Fe Jones

The truth about successfully stepping into your authentic self is that it's going to take courage. The people who have kept you in a box for so long will not be happy that you're growing beyond them. It will frustrate them that they can no longer control you.

I was always the helper, the assistant, the one people relied on to help make sure *their* dreams and goals came true. To step out on my own and take the risk to rise up and shine the way I was created to do is the best thing that's ever happened to me. And it will be the best thing that's ever happened to you too: if you let it be.

If you don't have enough belief in yourself just yet, borrow some of mine. I believe you were created for so much more than you're settling for. I believe that your people are waiting for you to show up authentically so they can be impacted by you. Your success is on the other side of your fear, if only you'll have the courage to go after it. I believe in you.

Come fly with me, friend.

ABOUT THE AUTHOR

Meggan Larson is a wife, mom, adoptee, course creator, entrepreneur, AFT Certified Success Coach, and a published author whose debut book The Truth About Forgiveness hit the number 1 new release spot in multiple categories.

She is passionate about helping women entrepreneurs succeed & serve from their authentic selves. She helps them transform from failure to success by teaching them how to believe in themselves unapologetically, find their voices, and fly.

If you are ready to transform your business, revolutionize your life, show up authentically, and impact the world, then head on over to her website at megganlarson.com, grab her free resources, join her online community, and fly with her.

2

THE TRUTH ABOUT DEFINING YOUR SUCCESS

LAUREN DA SILVA

This moment had been in the making for over five years. I sat beaming with pride in a two-hundred-year-old auditorium, dressed for the academic ceremony I had been waiting for nearly half a decade. Black cap and gown, with my bright orange sash on my lap, I was about to graduate my bachelor's degree with honors, cum laude—some of our class's highest grades.

"Lauren da Silva, cum laude!" I walked on stage and high-fived the air, turned to face the university president as she handed me my degree and placed my stole. I turned to face the crowd as they roared. Ululations, shouts and applause thundered down and poured over me from the crowd like confetti. This was a South African-style graduation ceremony if there ever was one.

I walked off the stage in tears, flashbacks from the past five years streaming through my mind automatically, as if it were reminding me of how far I had come, how hard I had worked, how I had *earned* this honor.

I completed my full-time course load on time and remotely

so I could stay in the workforce and pay my bills. Against all odds, I managed to juggle 3-4 jobs, my coursework, the rigorous internship requirements and intense travelling schedule. It cost my physical and mental health dearly, but I did it. I was standing there with my degree in hand, and I had *aced* it.

I had aced it even though nearly halfway through I had suffered an emotional breakdown which, in hindsight, was my body serving me notice that it had finally had enough. It wasn't going to enable my desperation for approval even a second longer. I pushed through, recovered (barely), and finished on time.

In between all this, I also got married, and was informed by my gynecologist that I wouldn't bear children without medical intervention, but I finished. *Cum laude.*

As I walked the stage, I felt my miracle flutter inside me: I was finally finished, *cum laude,* AND I was sixteen-weeks pregnant. The pride and joy just surged through my body in a moment that I would never forget. I was beaming...and deservedly so. I approached my family after the ceremony and walked straight to my dad. Finally, my moment had come. "Dad! Did you hear that? Cum laude! I graduated my honors degree *cum laude!*"

"I heard that, and if it was so easy for you, what I don't understand is why you couldn't just do *that* in high school. What an embarrassment!"

Gut punch.

My mountaintop. His humiliation of me.

The rain all over my victory parade. "You're *still* not enough, Lauren. I still see failure."

Every single one of my achievements has never been achievement enough.

An honors degree, cum laude. *Not enough.*

Ten years in ministry. *Not enough.*

Three beautiful children. *Not enough.*

An invitation and acceptance into a prestigious masters program. *Not enough.*

A bold and courageous move across the Atlantic. *Not enough.*

That moment perfectly captures the cold, dark and daunting shadow looming over any moment I am ever tempted to celebrate too hard. It's probably *still* not enough, isn't it?

It was never enough until one magical day the clouds in my mind parted, and I finally rebutted that stern, cold voice whose job it had been to keep me small and scared and asked, "Not enough *according to who?*"

Who gets to decide that it's not enough?

Why is their opinion more important than mine?

Why are their judgements and insecurities my ruler?

Who put their (ever-changing) definition of success in my dictionary?

The truth about success is that it is not objective.

Who will get to examine and define my achievements as successful or unsuccessful? I believe the only answer to that question is, "Me."

The truth about success is that if I ever want to enjoy anything I accomplish (and I may enjoy my accomplishments), I need to define what success means to me. That bar is mine, and mine alone to set.

The truth about success is that it is my responsibility to do the work of figuring out what living successfully will look like for me, and then it is my responsibility to live up to that standard.

The truth about success is that I need to choose how I would like to be remembered. I need to choose what being a successful wife or mother means. I need to choose what it means to use my time *successfully*. I need to choose what benchmarks I will use to measure *my* success.

Before I throw myself into the work of being a success, I need to throw myself into the work of defining it for myself. I also need to give myself permission to adjust my definitions as I go. I need to be okay with learning, growing and changing. I need to be okay looking back on what I once counted an achievement of a lifetime and calling it a mistake. I need to be okay with looking back at one of the hardest, most thankless and obscure seasons of my life and relabeling those "successes."

My moment on stage at my graduation ceremony is an example. It's been over a decade since that moment. I can look back on that time and the years leading up to it and know that it did indeed take an incredible amount of discipline and dedication to achieve what I did. I can also look back on that time and know that my dedication during those years was not to myself. I was completely dedicated to the shifting standards of people who thought that numbers on an academic report card represented a person's worth. I was sold out to the pursuit of validation from and approval of others. I wasted myself, caused irreparable damage to my body chasing the ever-moving mile markers of someone else's definition of success.

If I were aware of and had done the work of defining my own success in those years, I would have taken longer, been okay with lower grades, and would not have celebrated and worn my broken mind and body as a badge of honor.

Today, being able to like and love myself is success. Self-compassion is success. Margin and honoring my humanity are success. Giving it my best shot but holding that in tension with my other commitments is success.

Today I want a cum laude because I know that I am capable of one, and because I believe that to steward my mind towards doing its best thinking is owning and taking responsibility for my gifts. Today I know I don't want a cum laude at the expense of my faith and my family. I am okay with not gaining the world if I get to keep my soul.

Dearest reader, don't EVER give over the job of defining your successes to the people occupying the cheap seats of your life— or worse, the people who don't even have the courage to enter the auditorium with you. The people standing on the outside, on the edges of all the action shouting at you to do this or that, all while sitting on their lawn chairs, sipping their cocktails in the afternoon sun and talking about the people doing the things. These people with no skin in the game don't get to make or define the rules by which you play.

Don't ever let them convince you that where you are right now is success, failure, or obscurity. Only you get to call it that; and friend, please leave room in an increasingly black-and-white world for some grey, and better yet, make plenty of room for color.

One of the bravest things I have ever done is press pause on my career in graduate school (those value judgements on academic prowess are silent, but still very present to me) so that I could be the kind of mother I would remember one day and call *successful.*

I love my babies, but let's be real: Rearing children can be a pretty thankless task almost all the time. My choice to be a successful mother on my own terms has at times felt like a conflict of success with other areas of my life. I occasionally long to be back in the classroom, or for a vocation with office hours, where my contributions to the team are loudly and generously celebrated, where I can finally feel *enough.*

My definition of success anchors me in those moments, it reminds me that right now my presence has the most profound impact on a small crew of crazy humans, and that at least at this time I am pretty expendable in those other places. My definition of success also reminds me, in these very same moments, that I have permission to pursue my passions, and that to continue to nurture and develop them in spaces inside and around my motherhood is successful to me too.

Three years ago, "they" would ask me why I wasn't with my kids more, and now I get asked when I am going to start "using my potential." Their standards are always shifting, and let's be honest: in a crowd of spectators with very loud opinions, each person is going to have one. If it's unwise to adopt another's definition of success, it is absolute insanity to live for the approval of the entire crowd. That, I believe, is a recipe for pain, brokenness and true failure.

The truth about failure is that there isn't actually too much of it going around. My daughter likes to remind me that mistakes or missing the mark are simply invitations to make adjustments and try again. Every shot we miss is a step closer to the shot we'll make.

True failure is not missing the mark, it's never creating or establishing a mark of your own. True failure is setting your gaze and taking your aim to the mark of another. True failure is choosing to never load your bow, set your aim or take your shot. *Everything* else—every missed shot, every broken arrow, every frustrating blow—is a step closer to success, but it must start with *you* choosing *your own mark.*

The truth about success is that every single person reading this book has a different, completely subjective definition of it. Each and every one of us has a personal and unique goal. That is good, that is right, and it is true. Each and every one of us has a unique mission to accomplish and their very own mark to aim for.

My father has his own mark, a mark which he moves (and we all have permission to do this with our marks). I need to take responsibility for living and nearly dying to hit something that never belonged to me to begin with.

The past thirteen years of my life have been an exercise in learning to choose my own marks and making adjustments to them when they no longer serve me. They have been an exercise in taking full responsibility for the direction in which I am moving, and full responsibility for whether or not I get where I want to go. They have been an exercise in getting to know the incredible creative power bestowed upon me to get to where it is my purpose to go, and to start the work to get there.

I believe the same invitation beckons to you today.

Make your shot, but before you take your aim, make sure *you* have chosen your own mark.

ABOUT THE AUTHOR

Lauren da Silva is a wife, mother, writer, entrepreneur, and empath obsessed with learning as much as she can about the world and the people who live in it. She is a South African living in Waco, Texas and spends her free time creating or enjoying the outdoors. She dreams of a world where diversity is celebrated, where all who live in it feel safe and connected, and where we would choose to courageously turn toward one another & the messes we make in love, rather than fear.

Connect with her at https://laurendasilva.org

3

THE TRUTH ABOUT SUCCESS IN MOTHERHOOD

NATASHA LOOHUYS

"If only babies came with a manual."

I could feel the tight smile on my face and my forced chuckle as some well-meaning person responded to my sharing how the week's mothering had gone.

I knew that even the products that *do* come with manuals aren't comprehensive. Everyone always digs through the internet to "just make sure" they have all the information possibly available. At the time of my first born, I was in chat forums hourly for baby-burping techniques. Seriously, who tells a day-old mother that breastfed babies don't need burping? We found a bike-riding leg-action routine. Nailed it. Next item.

There was always something next. I was always working towards something.

Once we mastered burping, it was on to solid foods. Then it was longer naps, followed by walking, teething, talking. I vividly remember the intense relief when I was able to peel bubs away from me onto another surface, *and* he stayed asleep. "Feel for the limp arm," I was told. All of those milestones of success. Or so I thought.

I was so desperate to get to the next phase, whatever that was, that I never paused or took a breath and noticed what I had accomplished.

It had been three days since giving birth to our first baby. We were home; I was sitting, bleary-eyed, in the rocking chair, nursing, mindlessly swaying with the momentum of the chair, grateful for a moment of quiet. My husband, equally bleary-eyed and weary, was sitting on the floor and leaning against a wall. He was desperately trawling the internet for a discount code for a vasectomy. In that moment, I wanted that baby-rearing manual. I wanted to be told how to mother. I felt I was entirely out of my depth. I needed a checklist. My children would be screwed. This human was relying on me to be a successful mother. The judgement and opinions of others endlessly weighed on my heart and mind.

Could you imagine if babies did come with manuals? Imagine the additional to-dos and the how-to-dos for those to-dos. *Arggh.*

Fast forward six weeks.

My husband's annual leave was all gone. Our anxiety levels were at an all-time high. Bed, bath, book, boob, repeat. I was tired all over. I wished I had someone to ask what happened next, if I was getting motherhood right. I was afraid to ask anyone for fear of being told I was doing it wrong. My mindset was in the dirt.

As time passed, so did my passion. I called my husband's boss and politely suggested getting him back to work. He, too, was without joy and desperately needed some. I figured I could sort myself out later. I just needed to get through this part. Get through *this* phase.

My husband's work had him away from home half the time or more. My parents had died before my children were born. Each of my five sisters lived at least a five-hour flight away. My friendships before having babies had dwindled away. I felt alone. I was parenting without a village. I had turned into a person known only as "mother," filling everyone else's love buckets and not my own. This was how motherhood rolled for me. I was empty, weary, and resentful.

It took me eight years. Eight years to realize that I hadn't lost my passion; I just hadn't been present in it. My purpose and passion were not what or who I was before becoming a mother —it was being a mother.

A while passed before I owned my purpose and passion in motherhood. I was just living day to day; life was on repeat. No different from when my boys were babes in my arms. I was just getting through this phase, wishing and waiting for it to pass to get to the next one. That was my lightbulb moment. Why was I desperate to get through motherhood? Why was I so impatient to just get through this next phase?

It was fear.

I feared I had no idea what I was doing. I feared the people watching me were doing it better. I honestly felt there were no worthy successes from my time as a mother.

I would love to be dramatic and say time stood still for me in that moment and allowed me to relish the success of the mother I had become, but it didn't stand still. I was still working towards something. It was probably herding the boys out the door to school—but, in that moment of clarity, I realized I had been wishing away the reward of motherhood. I was not taking time to bask in the glory of all my motherhood successes. There was some self-sabotage in there, too, but that's a whole other story.

In that lightbulb moment, I realized that success is getting comfortable with the discomfort of the unknown; the unlearned and the broken norms of what mothering is or how society says it should be. Success is to follow my instincts, a mother's instincts. Success in motherhood isn't ticking items off that checklist I'd so dearly wished for.

I realized that in motherhood, success is to trust myself and believe in myself—that what I am doing in that moment, for the sole benefit of my children, is the right thing; becoming comfortable with that anxiety and fear of not knowing what the heck you are doing. That is success. And yes, it's terribly uncomfortable.

So much success in motherhood comes from being true to yourself, following your gut instincts and listening to your heart, not your head. There are so many well-intentioned people out there full of advice and support for our motherhood and parenting journeys that they dilute our own instincts. It creates so much grey for our own goals.

As a lifelong people-pleaser (that's an opening for another story), I followed the advice, and not necessarily for fear of not following it; it was for the fear of doing wrong by that person, not being loved by that person. But I wasn't doing right by me. I wasn't doing right by my children.

Now, years of hindsight prove to me that I was, and I am, a successful mother. Success in any career, including motherhood, is hard work, challenging, and sometimes very dirty. But when your hard work, bravery, and dirty work are your passion, you are in your purpose.

There is power in purpose. It gives meaning to your life. True happiness.

The next phase is now, and I am not eager for it to pass. I choose to relish all that I am taught in motherhood.

I choose to break the motherhood rules, too. Society has conditioned us to expect rewards, certificates, trophies, or money for a job well done. Can't we just bask in the joy it sparks in us? That's reward enough for me.

So, don't just rush off and start living passionately to feel purpose—to be that successful mother. It doesn't work like that. It needs to be *your* passion. Our passions shift as we live, grow, and age. So, it's not unusual that they also change and morph.

What calls you? What amazing gifts do you have? What is worth doing? Find your passion and then use it to serve. Serve family, friends, your community.

The grace I have granted myself to not rush motherhood is exhilarating. All the energy I had used worrying about the future (and that checklist) is now invested in living in my purpose. When I am in my purpose, I am living my passions. I am in service to others.

And, if you're curious, I now have spare time, too. Perfecting motherhood was time-consuming, mind-draining, and exhausting! I am now learning new hobbies, laughing more, listening more deeply, sharing more openly, and loving truly unconditionally.

If I live so passionately that I inspire my children to do the same, and they shine their passion and dreams on others, then I will have been an even greater success.

If the only thing we do is show our children to be passionate and dream big, then we have successfully impacted an entire generation for the better.

Get a (passion in) life.

Service is the rent we pay for living. It is the very purpose of life, and not something you do in your spare time.
—Marian Wright Edelman

ABOUT THE AUTHOR

Big heart, big solutions and big shoes (to fill).

Natasha Loohuys is a mother, mentor, personal coach, entrepreneur, author, public speaker and the one you come to for getting stuff done. A dynamic presence, curious and supportive, Natasha is community-centred, solution-focused, and has a thirst to engage everyone in the room. And she does it with gusto and passion! Being grounded and adventurous with *big* romantic ideas optimizes her to encourage and inspire. Purple steel-toes hung up for an apron, her purpose is now with her children and helping others. Whether she has implemented cost-savings on construction sites or is teaching children to knit, she is reliable and steady, sensitive and warm. Her passion is to show you how to be more resilient and positive, have energy and joy. Bring awareness to your day with more fun and less friction. So, reach out. She wants you to live in your purpose too!

Connect with Natasha here: www.natashaloohuys.com

4

THE TRUTH ABOUT SUCCESSFULLY OVERCOMING ENVY

CHRISTIANNA JOHNSON

I didn't want to be here.

"I" was a twenty-year-old college graduate with a career in medical lab technology ahead of me. "Here" was life. It wasn't that I wanted to die exactly. It was more that my life felt like a dull, colorless experience without joy or pleasure, and the thought of decades of feeling like that terrified me.

Up to that point, I'd lived my life as I was supposed to. Christ follower, choir girl, faithful church attendant, sober and zealous to good works. In a season of waiting, job interviews on the horizon, in perfect health.

But I wasn't happy. In fact, I am pretty sure I was depressed. The amount of sleeping and lack of feeling during that time could have been me recovering from months of clinical labs, studying and sleep deprivation. But without classes to attend, tests to study for, a goal and direction, I found myself in a space of nothing. No real feeling or drive. No desire or genuine happiness. And not really sure how I got here or if I'd ever get out. I just plainly didn't feel like I belonged *here* anymore, if I ever had.

But depression wasn't and isn't something really discussed or acknowledged in black independent Baptist churches. Either you're crazy or you're not, and I didn't seem crazy to people. But I sure didn't look like the happy and free glory-bound Christian I was supposed to be either.

At the time, I didn't know why. Especially when no one around me, no one I knew, seemed to be struggling the way I was.

Have you ever looked at others, knowing they were good people, and just felt "less than?" Felt seeds of envy and jealousy sprouting inside your gut? Have you looked at another person whom God seemed to be favoring over you and thought, "Wow, look who got all the goodies. Now I know how Cain must have felt."

Two things about me and Cain—we were so busy looking at our brother or our sister—another human—that we couldn't see ourselves. We couldn't see God and what He'd done for us. For me.

I wanted to be successful. To be good. To be happy. According to everyone around me, that meant going to college, getting good grades, doing impressive extracurriculars, and securing a stable career.

I wanted success, but I never wanted it like that. I never thought about what it looked like for me.

I knew what it looked like for other people. For the Other Girl. President of two clubs, taking ten classes at once, tutoring other students, in the college choir. Wonderful. Impressive. Not me, though.

The Other Girl seemed comfortable around people, well liked and happy even though she used up way more energy doing everything she did. Running meetings, clubs, being in choir. I could barely talk to the other people in my class.

No, I didn't know how to do that. I couldn't relate, couldn't get comfortable being around people, and couldn't connect. I could perform for a while, and I could get the grades, but I didn't have that same energy. My favorite places to be were the computer lab, writing stories, or tucked in a corner of the library reading.

What I thought was shyness and antisocial behavior was actual strong introversion and social anxiety—terms I wouldn't fully understand until years later. And my anxiety was so deep-seated and part of my functioning, I didn't realize how it controlled my decisions.

All I knew was that I wasn't like the Other Girls. I wasn't happy or good like them. I wasn't successful like them.

I was like me. But I didn't like me.

And that was a problem.

When I was a child, successful to me meant a day spent creating. Give me brushes and paint, glue and scissors, a box of crayons and colored pencils and a stack of paper. I'd spend hours creating something from some things and proudly present the final product to my mom. To this day, she has kept some of my scrawled drawings in a keepsake box.

While I was looking at the Other Girls and following the path of success, I put those creative days behind, thinking that they were less than. That I was less than for wanting something so simple and childish.

Artists weren't successful. There was a reason they call them "starving," and people like that had to live somewhere like New York or Los Angeles. People in Mississippi went to college, got a job, and that was that.

While other people were succeeding on this path, I was miserable. They were successful at being successful and were happy about it.

On top of anxiety and depression, I was envious. Envious of success and happiness that wasn't mine, I blocked what was for me. I took what was given to me, considered it worthless, and grasped at things that weren't mine. Being focused on someone else, I couldn't see what I had, what had been given to me to nurture.

If I feel envious of someone else, then I am sabotaging myself. I am delaying the things in my life that are for me.

Just because someone has something that I don't, it doesn't mean they are better. It does not mean that I am worse.

It is not a moral or value metric, and everyone is inherently worthy.

There is no space for judgement of either of us being good or bad. Learning how to release this judgmental stance of literally deciding someone else's cosmic moral alignment has been a task. It's inhuman. After doing years of work, I realized that judgement was not serving me.

I wasn't made to judge anyone. There's objectivity and discernment, but then there is judgement. We know the difference. And we have to let go of the role of judge if we want our success.

I never bought the seeds because I was too busy watching her and critiquing how deeply she dug the holes and why she chose those flowers. She should have planted a vegetable or something edible. That's what I would do.

At the end of the season, she is reaping the bounty of things she has sown and tended to. I am not. My garden is full of weeds, the few good seeds planted choked out and neglected.

I had to change, to grow. My mindset had to be renewed, and old thinking had to die.

The seeds of comparison and competition were planted in me as a child.

She didn't mean to, but these seeds didn't yield good fruit. Maybe that's how my grandmother raised her, maybe it helped her. Likely she didn't know better. Whatever seed she meant to plant, these are the ones that rooted:

I am not good enough as I am.

I don't know enough.

Who I am is not good.

Who I am is not enough.

I must know more, do more, to receive love and praise.

If I perform better, behave better, I will be safe.

If I know what to do, then I can do it when I need to and I will be safe.

I never realized all these seeds were in me. Not just in me, but growing and bearing fruit. I was judgmental. I was envious and jealous, disdainful of people.

Journaling showed me this. My thoughts were so plainly written out in my own hand, easily taken apart and examined in stark black letters.

The examination set me off on a journey of self-care, though I didn't call it that at the time. Self-care is trendy with ideas of home spa days, manicures with vegan, non-toxic nail polish, and luxurious splurges. Nothing wrong with that at all, of course, and I do it too.

But this self-care was ugly. This self-care looked more like digging through my heart and thinking. There, I unearthed dark weeds of hate, judgement, bitterness, unforgiveness, envy, jealousy, sadness, fear...so much fear.

Some enemy had sown these seeds, I'm sure, and a hideous garden had grown up inside of me.

It was scary to be confronted with such dark things—not *me*, but *in* me, rooted deep down. And it's not as though the garden was dead.

These things were growing, thriving. The fruit they yielded was toxic, tolerable to a point before the body sickened and died. The dying could take a while, years stretched out in pain and misery.

This garden was so full of poison that it would kill anyone. Kill any thought of hope or happiness, of success and prosperity. No wonder I struggled. All the resources—love, time, energy—

that should have gone to growing rich fruits were feeding deadly things.

The self-care I had to go through looked like grieving. It looked like sobbing for hours in the middle of the night as I released old pain I never processed. I wept over and forgave myself for taking wounds and judging myself. I forgave myself for not knowing. I forgave others who never meant to hurt me. I spoke the truth of what happened to me and of how my life had slipped out of my control.

And then I ripped out the garden.

When you are jealous and when you are comparing, you invalidate the gifts and talents you've been given. I nurtured my talents, and when I reaped my harvest, I chose gratitude. I didn't look at anyone else, or like anyone else. I didn't compare or judge. I reaped goodness and gave thanks.

Be grateful for your path and your journey. Define your vision, set your goals, break them down into projects, and write them in your planner. Move forward. Be grateful for who you were, who you are now, and who you are becoming. That you have your infinite possibilities to choose from and trust the future is not something to fear.

If my Father, being good, loves me, and I ask Him having faith, then He will give me everything good that is for me. And if I ask and do not receive, then I've asked amiss; the thing I thought was good was not meant for me.

He is a good, good Father. He knows what He's doing. And He cares for me.

Take these thoughts and plant them like seeds.

You are good. You are worthy. When you really believe that you are good as you are, that you always have been, then you won't feel the need to look at someone else and envy their good-ness—you have your own.

Connect with what your desires are. When I connected with what I wanted, it ended up looking very familiar. My desires looked like everything I'd wanted as a child—to make things. To create. To spend days making something that didn't exist before I encountered it. It is a simple desire and simply a joy.

That want was a seed sown into me before I was born, when I was wonderfully made.

It's okay if you don't know or don't remember what you want. May you receive light and clarity in your seeking. And in your seeking, find. Be sincere and diligent in your search. Don't shrink back from what you discover.

It might be uncomfortable and strange. It might make you weep. But it is good. If you are hurting, then you are in the process of healing and growing. We can't heal a hurt we don't feel.

If you want to be successful, then you have to define that for yourself. You have to know what you want for your life—not what someone else told you was what you wanted. The dreams and desires that God planted in you only need a little nurture, but it's deliberate work. Sometimes it's painful work.

If you want to be successful, you have to be grateful. Otherwise, you'll never care about what you have, never be satisfied.

Choose to make it fun and easy. Choose to rest in this prayer —the God who brought you in, who formed you and foreknew you, who loves you: This God will lead you through all the days of your life; this God fully equipped you to live life as He intended; and this God will never let anything separate you from His love.

I have low moments, but not so often. And I have hope for all the days of my life. My success is mine. My good is for me, and I am grateful. All the blessings in your endeavors. They're already yours.

ABOUT THE AUTHOR

Christianna Johnson has written for over a decade, spanning from creative nonfiction, to fantasy and science fiction. Introvert and investigator, she has been dedicated to researching tips and trends of self publishing and building a community of like minded writers like herself as founder of The Introverted Writers Club. She is an avid reader, blogger at bychristianna.com, course creator of Boundaries for Creatives, an Enneagram enthusiast, and author of and amateur podcaster of *Made to Create*.

5

THE TRUTH ABOUT SUCCESSFULLY OVERCOMING OVERTHINKING

DAWN SHANNON

For years I played it safe.

As a Loyal Enneagram[1] 6, fear was the driving force for many of my decisions in life. But it hadn't always been that way.

After flunking out of college, I went back home and needed to work. A few blocks away was the local movie theatre where I accidentally (or divinely) showed up on the exact day another person was scheduled for an interview. She was late, so they thought I was her. After explaining I wasn't her (or late), they interviewed me anyway and I got the job!

I started out in Concessions and was very good at my job. I was eager, confident, and determined to move up the ranks quickly—which I did. I went from "popcorn girl" to general manager in a very short period of time. My confidence couldn't be shaken.

After ten years in the movie-theater business, working three jobs and going back to school to get my associate's degree, I was tired of working nights, weekends, and holidays, so I decided to look for a "real job." There are many twists and turns in my journey, but I ultimately ended up working for a small architectural firm as their only administrative assistant. At first there was a lot to learn about the industry, but I learned quickly and became their go-to gal for just about anything they needed in the office, including administrative work, human resources and marketing. I did it all!

I stayed with that company for almost fifteen years. Can you see a pattern here?

Again, I was in a position where I was extremely confident in what I was doing and was very good at it, but as time went on I knew *I was meant for more.*

Throughout my journey I had always been that person other people sought out for advice. When employees, friends or co-workers were in a tiff, they would come to me as a mediator to help resolve the problem.

As time went on, I heard about the professional coaching industry and had a cousin who became a certified coach. After hearing her talk about it for a while, I thought, "That's what I do anyway, why not make a living out of it?" I followed her lead and became a certified professional coach.

I was still working at the architectural firm but quickly realized I wanted more.

While networking, I met a fiery redhead who was a massive Visionary. I was the Integrator to her Visionary (think yin and yang). We teamed up to start a brick-and-mortar business, and after a few months of planning, the business was open. She worked there daily, and I continued working my full-time, steady job.

Then, the unexpected happened. My mom died!

She suffered from an undiagnosed brain tumor. Once discovered, she started treatment, but unfortunately it was too late. She only lived two more months. Within one year I went from being on Cloud 9, finally stepping out in faith to start a new business, to experiencing the most devastating loss in my life at that time: losing my only parent—my mom.

That's when it all began.

The fear, doubt, second-guessing, not knowing what to do... It was horrible! I was a single mom of a young man about to graduate from high school and his "Nahni" wouldn't be there to watch him cross the stage and receive his diploma. I would have NEVER expected that!

At that moment I decided that life was too short, and I quit my J-O-B. I started working with my business partner and things were going well, until the overthinking crept in.

As a Visionary, my business partner had so many great ideas and wanted to implement them all right away. As the Integrator, I needed more information like:

- How would this work?
- Where's the money coming from?
- How will we get clients?
- What if we fail?

And on, and on it went, until my overthinking was too much for the partnership. I doubted myself, felt overwhelmed and overshadowed most of the time, so I left. With my head hung low in shame, although putting on a brave face, I decided that coaching was what I was meant to do, so that's what I did.

Even that proved to be challenging at first.

When I decided to take the leap of faith and go out on my own, I lost the structure and safety net I was used to. As a solopreneur, I felt isolated and confused about what to do next. I was unclear about who I was meant to serve. I knew what I wanted but it didn't seem possible. My vision for my future was cloudy, and I doubted my ability to pursue it.

I knew I was meant for more, but really knowing what that meant became a struggle. I began doing the things that other entrepreneurs said to do, networking and posting on social media, but nothing seemed to be working.

What I came to realize was that I needed to get very clear about why I was pursuing this dream of being an entrepreneur. I needed a clear vision I could believe in!

I tried time and time again to tap into my ideal client, but there always seemed to be obstacles getting in the way. I couldn't visualize how to help them in a way that honored my heart AND make the kind of money I wanted to make.

Then comes another firecracker into my life who taught me that being heart-centered in business is doable.

Martha Krejci showed me how to visualize what I wanted and how to make it work as a business. Through her mentoring I realized *I was the barrier to my success*. I have since learned how to shift my mindset and **believe** in my ability to do what God called me to do.

And I've created a **VISION** for my success I can finally **believe in!**

Having a very clear, holistic vision I could believe in was what I needed to push through the fear, doubt and second-guessing.

This began my journey to success.

Next, it was time to get in alignment with my values.

Values are the things in life you consider most important. Even though I thought I knew what my core values were, I needed to be sure.

For most people, values are established at an early age within our family. My immediate family consisted of my mother, stepfather and brother, but we also spent a lot of time with our grandparents and great aunt and uncle.

The values I learned from them were conflicting to say the least.

Should I work hard for one company all my life hoping they would take care of me in retirement? That happened for my grandparents, so that's what they believed in.

Should I stay in a volatile relationship, walk on eggshells and hope it gets better? That's what my mom did.

Should I go to church even though my parents didn't? My great aunt thought so. She picked up me and my brother every week for church.

It was very confusing!

I needed to know what *my values* were.

During my coach training, I took a *Values Assessment*[2] that helped me learn more about values: what they were, what they meant for me and how to choose which ones I wanted to live by. It also showed me that when I live according to my core values, every decision becomes easier.

So there I was, still on the entrepreneurial journey. I finally knew my WHY and figured out my **VALUES**. I was making decisions in alignment with those values but there was still a missing piece: *ACTION!*

That's when my motto was born...

A plan *without* ACTION is a DREAM DEFERRED!

~Dawn Shannon

Like the sound a car makes as it revs its engine preparing to take off, it was time for me to make my own noise. *VROOM!*

Like so many others, I would dream about the kind of success I wanted but would find it hard to take action. I was overthinking every decision!

So, what changed?

I allowed people into my life to hold me accountable to the things I said I wanted to do, and I started taking consistent, intentional, and doable action. This small group of supportive women helped me see my strengths and encouraged me to take action despite my fears.

Through this process, I figured out a strategy that helped me with any and every decision. I ask myself three key questions:

* Was what I wanted to do in alignment with the Vision I had for my life and business?

* Was it in alignment with my Values?

* Was I willing and able to take consistent, intentional, and doable action?

If the answer was "YES," I took action—*Vroom*. If the answer was "NO," I felt good about that decision—no more second-guessing.

When I became obedient and implemented this strategy, everything changed. I figured out my messaging, I started attracting my tribe, and I finally started feeling good about myself!

I knew I had to share this strategy with other overthinkers, so I created the '**V³ Strategy**': **VISION, VALUES & VROOM.** Now I help other women to stop overthinking and start doing despite their fears.

We are all on a unique journey, and the path to success is different for everyone. For some, the path is illuminated more brightly because they see what they want clearly and go for it. For others, like me, it might take a little longer to reach because past experiences have taught us to be more cautious.

Once I decided what I had to offer was valuable and figured out how to stop overthinking and start doing despite my fear, my journey to the truth about my success became clear—and that feels so good!

My friend, if you have a dream in your heart that has been there for a long time, isn't it time to stop deferring that dream? I hope your answer is "yes," but more importantly, I hope you will find your small, supportive group and make a commitment to yourself to *stop overthinking and start doing!*

ABOUT THE AUTHOR

Certified Professional Coach, Dawn Shannon, works with women who are visionaries, entrepreneurs and all-around go-getters who are tired of overthinking every doggone decision and ready to start doing.

As a former overthinker, Dawn spent years overthinking every decision which drove the people around her crazy! It was even the root cause of her walking away from her first business venture as an entrepreneur with her head hung low in shame.

Dawn has finally found the formula that helps her take doable action every day without overthinking every decision and confidently shares her strategy with others so they too can *Stop Overthinking and Start Doing*!

Connect with her at www.jovistrategies.com

II

LOSS & RESILIENCE

6

THE TRUTH ABOUT LIVING AGAIN AFTER LOSING THE LOVE OF YOUR LIFE

ROSILAH SANI

My oldest son turned eighteen a few months ago. In that moment, I realized I had been holding my breath for fifteen years and could finally heave a big sigh of relief. Yes, this young man was going to be fine. And his brother too, despite a very shaky start in life after losing their beloved father.

Watching him blow out his birthday candles as we celebrated with family and friends, my heart was bursting with every imaginable happy emotion. Shortly after, he was accepted into his chosen field at the University of New South Wales, and I knew my boy was on the cusp of making his mark in the world.

The poignancy hit me only later while scrolling through the photos of the party and remarking once again on his incredible resemblance to his father. Joy was tinged with a deep sadness of how proud his father would have been to see him now.

Have you ever had a dream come true after such a long time that you had even forgotten about it, and had the realization of that dream become one of the most bittersweet moments in your life?

On a lazy hang-out-with-a-girlfriend kind of day, ruminating on what we wanted to achieve in life, I announced that all I wanted was to have a child and raise him or her to be a good, responsible person, someone who would make a contribution to this world, though not necessarily in a major way. Just a good person.

At the time, I was in a long-distance relationship fraught with cultural and religious differences, challenged by different time zones in an era before Skype, WhatsApp or FaceTime. With me working in Canada and him living in Italy, communications were by phone, email, or snail mail. The odds were against us. With a few failed relationships behind me, there was no reason to think that this would be any different.

The story of how we met was incredible enough: I moved from Singapore to a job in the Netherlands with a strong desire to experience life in other countries. He was in the same institution for a postgrad course. We moved in the same groups. By the time the friendship blossomed into more, I had already accepted another job in Vancouver and was determined to put this relationship behind me as well, but he had other ideas. It took a few more years and much anguish but, in the end, love conquered all.

Our first son was born six days after my forty-third birthday: two weeks late, perfect, beautiful, and healthy. The umbilical cord had been tangled around his neck and it took an emergency C-section to save him. My husband said he'd lost ten years of his life while I was in the operating room. (That remark will haunt me for the rest of my life.)

Our second son arrived two years later, as beautiful and healthy as his brother. They were—in the words of our paediatrician—"little miracles." The risk of genetic diseases was high because of my age and the medical history in my husband's family, triggering higher-than-normal anxieties throughout both pregnancies. But we overcame the odds. We were in seventh heaven, planning for a third, hoping it would be a girl. The world was my oyster! Until it all came crumbling down just before our little one's first birthday.

One minute my husband and I were happily setting up the new furniture in the boys' bedroom while they were with the grands, and the next he was on the floor, surrounded by paramedics.

They could not resuscitate him.

Over the next few days our small apartment was filled with people paying their respects. The following weeks were a blur, surrounded by good friends and relatives, family from Singapore, old friends from the Netherlands. On my own, I would listen for the sound of the key turning in the door, watch to catch a glimpse of his head walking down the steps of our apartment building, willing to meet him in my dreams, although in those dreams he was always just out of sight or out of reach.

WHY HIM, GOD????!!!! Why? It's not fair! He had so much going for him. Who's going to take the boys canoeing on the Colorado River now?!

That was our big plan as soon as they were old enough. An up-and-coming professor in his university and respected by colleagues internationally, he was an ardent geologist who traveled for his profession, with me tagging along, fascinated to see the world through his eyes. We went snorkeling at the Great Barrier Reef of Queensland, braved icy slopes to touch the Delicate Arch in Arizona (I was certain we would fall to our deaths), took an overnight mule ride to Phantom Ranch at the bottom of the Grand Canyon (one misstep and you're down there before everyone else), drove ten hours with our two-month-old on Italy's winter highways to the ski slopes of Marilleva (with a breastfeeding stop every two hours!), and so much more.

He had a zest for life like no other person I knew. He would laugh away my fears, and I trusted him implicitly with my life. No one could fathom the depth of my grief, not even me. When someone remarked, "I know how you feel. I just lost my mother," or "I just lost my husband too," I would be screaming inside.

No! You don't know how I feel! I just lost the love of my life! I'm living in a country where I speak the language like a tourist, my little boys will never experience again the immense love of their father, their grandparents are so completely devastated that they can't even mention their son's name!

None of those emotions surfaced. My inner person wanted to curl up in a corner and shrivel away to nonexistence, but I had to be strong for my children to the best of my ability. I was determined they should have the lifestyle their father would have provided.

"I've got this!" or so I thought.

Before my marriage, I was a successful, independent career woman. In a poor family of fourteen children, my father had always challenged us to do our best. I became the first woman graduate in Surveying in New South Wales—this little Asian girl (my classmates' description) who held her own among the "blokes," her professors' wives attending her graduation ceremony to show solidarity.

Back home, I worked for the government as the first woman graduate surveyor, a proud representative of our minority Malay community, before moving to the commercial sector, establishing a profession in the emerging Information Sciences—often at the leading edge of technology—traveling and living around the world.

I had flown in the face of gender and racial biases. Plus, I was an aunt many times over, with years of experience helping to care for my siblings' children. I could raise two boys on my own! We continued to enjoy our Sunday promenades, the golden sands of South Italian beaches in summer, fun excursions with friends. Deep inside, it was torture for me to see couples with their complete happy families, but I never voiced this. At the end of the day, it was just the three of us saying goodnight to Daddy's star in the sky.

Despite striving for normalcy after an "acceptable" grieving period, in the back of my mind was always the question: *Who would care for the boys if anything happened to me?* I became paranoid about my own mortality. I packed everything up and moved halfway around the world to Sydney with a three-year-old and a five-year-old in tow, driven away by the struggling Italian economy and the need to be closer to my family, leaving their sad grandparents behind.

Sydney was this vibrant city by the sea. The promise of a new, exciting job and a fresh new life for us was irresistible. The boys, with their adorable Italian accents, would be spoiled by their relatives.

In reality, the next ten years were a roller coaster of deep, dark places and bright, happy times. Chronic pain, invisible illnesses, daily medications under specialist care, conflicts at work and at home, fighting at school—it all took its toll. I was stressed, overwhelmed, and spiralling, battered by forces outside of my control. *What was the point of this life?*

The catalyst for change was knowing that I had to **be** the change for my sons, to mend the breaks in our existence before they became irreparable.

Eventually stumbling upon my path to healing, the pent-up grief came flooding out one day as though a dam had burst. Then, seemingly innocent memories all the way back from my childhood resurfaced. The brain weaves your perceptions of events into a version of what happened, and whether true or not, these are the stories that you hold on to, subconsciously.

The keystone of my healing was connecting with that little girl—my inner child—to set her experiences in perspective, deepening my faith to let go of fear and control. The transformation inside me was palpable, from erratically emotive to calm and collected; from aggressive to assertive.

I am finding my voice. I am relaying my story here for the first time in the hope that this telling encourages you, my dear reader, to embrace your inner child and your emotions, for there are no bad emotions, only bad reactions.

Time heals all wounds, they say. Well, not quite. The scar remains—the loss, the longing that still hurts when you touch it. Have I overcome the grief? No, because numbing the grief would also numb me to the wonderful emotions intrinsically linked to it. Grief is marbled into my being, and I draw upon it when compassion, empathy, and forgiveness are called for. Starting with myself.

If I could, I would go back to assure that little girl, and others like her, that:

It's ok to not be like others.

It's ok to admit that you've been hurt by words or actions.

It's ok to speak up and not continue to please others by your silence.

It's ok to draw the line and say to them, "You've crossed it, and I choose not to let you do it again."

It's ok to not always be strong or always right or always the best.

It's ok to put yourself first sometimes, even if it means handing your responsibilities to someone else temporarily.

It's ok to ask for help when you need it, and to keep looking for it in the right places.

"Help" is the hardest, and the bravest, thing to say.

I know that it is in you to do all of the above if you can stop in your tracks for a minute, take stock of your current direction and the destination you are headed in, and ask yourself, "Is that where I truly want to go?"

The truth is: Success is not marked by worldly achievements, by how others celebrate you, nor by vicarious pleasure in the accolades given to those you support. These are hollow when **you** have not appreciated your own worth.

Embrace your real self, recognize your value, regain the balance and resilience to turn the pain that life throws at you into purpose, savor the freedom of living your own choices and letting your voice be heard. These make you unstoppable in the pursuit of your goals and vision.

Then, look in the mirror to see what success truly is.

ABOUT THE AUTHOR

Rosilah is a Scientist, Educator, Coach, and Founder of The AromaQi Method. She has a fascination for neuroscience and the heart-brain connection, finding insights in their synergy with the ancient modalities of Qigong & Aromatherapy to aid in healing the mind, body, and spirit. She now dedicates her rejuvenated golden years to helping stressed & overwhelmed career mums regain the balance, resilience, & freedom to live their best lives. Is there a voice inside you, an inner person that wants to be heard? Are you stuck and struggling, wishing you could find your purpose and direction in life? Then head over to A Sanricco Life at www.sanricco.com for community support, information and resources. Together we can write a better future for our children and their children.

"Do ... or do not. There is no try." Yoda

7

THE TRUTH ABOUT SUCCESSFULLY HEALING AFTER CHILDHOOD LOSS

NATALIE RODRIGUEZ

T*RIGGER ALERT — This chapter deals with the loss of a parent and suicidal thoughts.*

She wasn't going to make it.

The room spun around me as I curled up on the floor and wept. At just fourteen years old, instead of worrying about the girls at school, my latest crush, or what grade I had gotten on my last history test, I was being suffocated with the news that my mom wasn't going to wake up from the coma she'd been in for the last two weeks. She was going to die, and there was nothing I could do about it.

It had started seven months earlier, with some numbness on one side and a seizure while driving. She had surgery to remove the tumor. That's when they found that it was cancerous and started chemo. The six months that followed were full of hair loss, exhaustion, and a whole lot of pretending that everything would be okay. But here we were, staring in the face of what no one wanted to admit was a possibility until now.

I'd gone to visit her just once since she'd gone into the hospital. It was summer, but my dad was working full time and visiting hours didn't make it easy, I guess. The details of that visit are fuzzy, but I remember there were several people in the room with us, and I was uncomfortable and scared. Someone, maybe my dad or grandma, told my little sister and me that we could talk to our mom, hold her hand, tell her we loved her, that she could hear us.

I took her hand but couldn't speak. It was so swollen, almost like there was a balloon under her skin, and I didn't understand why. I could feel the eyes on us, and the vulnerability was so thick in the air I was nearly choking on it. I didn't want these people to see my pain or my fear. I wanted to be brave and stoic, but in reality I was frozen. I must've known on some level how serious this was, but my brain wasn't yet willing to accept it. I would regret that moment for the next twenty years of my life.

After realizing I might've seen my mom for the last time, I eventually cried myself out and went to bed. Before I fell asleep, I prayed harder and with more desperation than I ever had in my short little life. I didn't even pray for God to make her better, to heal her. I simply prayed that I could fix my "mistake" and tell her I loved her one last time before she was gone. It was a Saturday, and it would've been the perfect opportunity to visit her, which gave me hope.

The next morning, before I could see her and say all the things that were on my heart, she passed away.

I sat with that shame and regret for a long time, and I refused counseling. I used to wish and wonder if it was all just a dream or a prank. As cruel as it would've been, I longed for the words that would never come. "Just kidding, she's fine!"

I was in a dark place for years. I didn't have any formal diagnosis because I refused counseling. The internet wasn't much of a thing back then, so I didn't have the resources to understand that I was experiencing grief, anxiety, and depression.

I was angry too. That was the overlying emotion of that period of my life. Angry with God, angry with myself, angry at life, and at the world. I had so much hate and anger festering inside of me. My dad and I fought constantly and the pressure to keep it together for my sister was overwhelming. I felt like I was the closest thing she had to our mom at that point, and I tried to be strong for her, but deep down, I longed for death. I just wanted the pain to go away, but I knew I'd never do it. How could I take another loved one from my family when I knew the pain of losing someone so deeply? I thought about running away and I even wrote letters and hid them under my bed. I just needed an escape from the pain.

That's when I discovered self-harm. I started in high school by digging my nails into my ankles, where it wouldn't be easily seen. I stopped for a while in college by replacing it with drinking and drugs. Anything to feel better, even if just for the moment.

When things started getting rocky with my boyfriend, and even rockier with my dad, I started cutting again, using a razor blade this time. It was a temporary escape from what I now know were severe panic attacks. Focusing on that physical pain made the emotional pain fade and gave me the release I needed to start breathing again. But it was always temporary. I stopped with my next boyfriend because he asked me to, and I really liked him, but those urges were still there, lurking just beneath the surface.

Instead, my panic attacks led to holes in doors and walls. I still needed that release of pain, and I still hated myself deep down. No matter what I achieved, no matter how much I tried to "be a better person," I still carried that weight of shame and guilt.

Several years later, I started working for a woman I now realize was a narcissist who was gaslighting me. At the time, all I knew was that the way she treated me, micromanaging and talking down to me, triggered me in a big way. I started having daily panic attacks, crying in the bathroom at work several times a week, just trying to catch my breath so I could finish my shift.

By then I was a mom, and my toddler was triggering me weekly as well. Anything I couldn't control or that didn't go as planned would set me off. It came to a head when I got so angry with my toddler that I threw his chair several feet away and flipped over his table in a fit of rage because he wouldn't listen to me. My toddler wouldn't listen to me. That's what they do, isn't it? But I couldn't deal.

It was then I realized how lost I was, and how badly I needed help. I was afraid the only thing that would help at that point would be an in-patient program, but I didn't even know where to start. A friend mentioned that she was seeing a therapist to heal from the abuse her ex had put her through, so I asked her for a referral. What did I have to lose?

That first visit was so hard. I'd dabbled in therapy for several years, never really making it through to the root issue. When things would start to get too painful, I would run. I saw some crappy therapists too. One even shamed me when I admitted that I had started cutting myself again. (One thing you need to know about therapy is that you have to find the right therapist for you. Just like you won't be everyone's cup of tea in this world, and everyone won't be yours, every therapist won't work for every patient. You have to find the right fit. But when you do, it can make a world of difference.)

Reliving that moment in the hospital was painful. So was digging up all the pain, realizing how angry I was at my dad for the way he didn't grieve in front of us, for the way he changed after she died, for not waiting "long enough" to start dating again, for picking someone we didn't (at the time) approve of, for not being what I needed, not providing the emotional support I needed, not giving me more opportunities to visit my mother in the hospital.

My therapist had me write a letter to him, telling him all the ways I admired and appreciated him. In that same time period, I attended a self-help seminar where I learned how to forgive, and worked through forgiving myself for my missed opportunity, and forgiving God for not giving me what I had begged for. Those two things were the turning point for me. I finally felt a little relief and hope that the future could be less painful than the past twenty years had been. It didn't happen overnight, but little by little things started to get better.

That was close to five years ago. There are still days when I struggle, days when that past pain bubbles back up to the surface, when I find a new thing triggering me. But now I have hope, and tools to work through those triggers and memories.

You see, the truth about successfully healing from childhood loss, and healing in general, is that it is incredibly messy. Sometimes we are fed these pretty pictures of healing in movies and media and expect life to be happy-go-lucky after a few months in therapy or meeting a special person that makes life worth living.

Real life isn't like that.

The truth is, I'll probably always be healing. Each new chapter of our lives uncovers a new layer of pain, resentment, and grief. And then the forgiveness and healing begin again. You just have to keep on trying, in whatever messy way you can. Find a good therapist, seek community, learn to forgive, and to take care of yourself emotionally.

The real key to healing, and the most important part, is to never ever give up.

ABOUT THE AUTHOR

Natalie is a wife, and mom to one, with another on the way. After losing her own mother at the age of 14, she struggle through 20 years of anxiety, depression, and suicidal thoughts (or she spent 20 years battling mental health struggles) before ultimately finding the right combination of tools to work through her grief and shame. Now she helps others in similar situations to identify their own root issues that are holding them back and sabotaging their lives, in order to process their grief, forgive, and experience a life of hope and freedom. She currently runs a Facebook support group and offers 1:1 coaching sessions, and also has a podcast and book in the works.

Connect with Natalie here: healyoursoul.net

8

THE TRUTH ABOUT SUCCESS AFTER LOSING YOUR DREAMS

JENNA HERRIG

I had always been excited about the idea of motherhood. From the moment my first doll was placed in my arms as a child, I could hardly wait to be a mommy. I had everything all planned out. That is, of course, until the day I was told we would never have children.

Friday the 13th was when we were given the devastating news. My heart was shattered, and thus began my season of deep sadness. I was absolutely blindsided by the news and could have never predicted that it was coming.

My husband Clinton and I were married in 2011 on a gorgeous June day. We had dreamed about starting a family, but we knew we wanted at least two to three years of just being a couple, living life, and experiencing adventures together. I was on birth control for just a little over a year, and sometime after our one-year anniversary we decided to try for a baby. I had previously read an article that women who were on my birth-control plan had a very hard time conceiving. Reading that information made me a little worried. We both agreed that this could take a year or a little more, and we tried not to worry.

A year went by and no baby—not even a late or missed period. Clinton reassured me that all was okay. Sometimes it took couples just a little longer to have a baby. Plus, we both really didn't like going to the doctor. Don't get me wrong, we LOVE that there are amazing doctors in the world; we just always dread visiting them.

Another year went by and still no baby. We were a little concerned, but we decided we were just going to commit to prayer as best as we could and work on staying calm and taking care of our bodies. Being a curvy woman, I thought maybe I just needed to lose some weight. I started working out and eating clean whole foods. Guess what? Another year was approaching, and I told Clinton we needed to make the appointment. It was time.

We met with our doctor and shared with him what was going on and that we were nervous for the next step. The next step was finding out why we are unable to conceive and what was causing it to happen. In our minds, it meant something was wrong with one of us or perhaps even both of us.

In the summer of 2014, we started going through lots of tests. And by November (Friday) 13th, 2014 we received a letter that stated that our doctor was so sorry, but there was no chance of us ever conceiving naturally. I read that letter and instantly began sobbing. I have tears in my eyes just from revisiting this memory.

After reading the letter, I retreated to my bed and Zoey, my sweet English springer spaniel, followed me closely. I lay down on my side of the bed and curled up; Zoey just put her head by mine. She knew I was hurting. She was such a sweetheart to me in those next few days and weeks. Dogs know when we are broken and sad. They are such a great comfort.

My bed became the place where I felt the safest. It was the place I could just quietly lie and only focus on breathing. I imagined myself crumbling to broken pieces if I simply stood up. I would get up a time or two, of course; I'd go to the bathroom or sit in the chair by the window and just stare blankly outside. My house soon became my sanctuary, a place I didn't ever want to leave. It was like my house just engulfed me in its embrace and I could feel a hundred percent safe there.

After about two weeks, Clinton softly suggested that it was time for me to go back to my part-time job. Fear set in big time. Anytime I left my house, I was extra emotional; it was a guarantee that I would be crying at some point during the day. Sometimes the emotions would hit when I was sitting in my car, just trying to muster the strength to go into a store.

I knew Clinton was right, though. I knew that if I didn't rise from my bed, it would swallow me whole and I would be lost to who I was for a very long time. I'm so thankful I have Jesus in my life. I knew He was there the whole time. I prayed daily for Him to comfort me. I would pray, "Fill me with your joy, Lord," and I would just weep. I remember minutes after reading that letter, I prayed that God would not allow me to let jealously or anger dwell in my heart. I believe an extra dose of sadness settled in, but I was okay with that. I knew I could handle the extra sadness, tears, and headaches from crying so much. I was and still am SO thankful that jealousy and anger were not an issue for me.

Is anger and jealousy something you are struggling with? It's okay to embrace it. Just don't let it sit and fester for long because it will eat you up, spit you out and eat you all over again. That's not a cycle you want to reside in, dear friend. Pray to Jesus for help, talk to a highly trusted friend, journal, or meditate.

One of my blessings is that I work for my dad's company. I am a part-time secretary, and I get to work closely with my mom. My mom is an office manager, and I am like her personal secretary.

I arrived at work, and this was the first time my mom saw me after I shared the news with her over the phone. I managed to make it through a few hours at work and then, all of a sudden, tears were just streaming down my face. She came over and wrapped her arms around me. She asked if I was okay. I shared with her and said, "I'm so sad all the time. The sadness won't go away. I'm starting to get embarrassed that I'm so sad because I didn't lose an actual baby. People will think I have lost my mind."

You know what she told me? She said, "You are allowed to grieve. You are mourning. You lost your hopes and your dreams. Now you are learning what's next. And that's scary. It's okay to feel that way." I will never forget her words. It was like Jesus himself was speaking through my sweet mom and came out and touched my soul. I was so grateful to her in that moment. I still couldn't stop the tears flowing, but she made me feel like it was a hundred percent okay that I was feeling that way.

I want to say that to you too. You are allowed to grieve. Wherever you are on your journey, whether you are mourning the loss of a dream, the loss of a child, the loss of a parent, the loss of a job, the loss of who you are—this is not the end. Allow yourself time to grieve and mourn. It is the very first step in your healing journey. It's not always pretty, but I promise it is worth it. If you need a friend, then hold on to my hand, hold on to Jesus. You are going to be okay.

Restoring my hope and discovering my joy again took time. While journeying through my sad season, I learned how to create a morning routine to help me set up my day for success. I thought if I could do just one simple thing in the morning for myself, then I knew I was making progress on the first steps of my healing journey. I began journaling and writing down three to five things that I was grateful for. Each day I would try to write down different things that I was grateful for. Some days it was something as simple as being thankful the sun was shining and the flowers were blooming.

Give yourself time to reflect on how you are feeling. Begin a gratitude journal and write what you are feeling. Where are you feeling it in your body? Where does it hurt? I always seem to feel the emotion in my chest or my stomach. Just feel it wherever it is. Tell yourself, "Hey sadness," or "Hey fear...I feel you. I see you. I accept you. We are okay. God is taking care of us."

Let yourself journal today, meditate on God's word, read a motivational book, look up your favorite inspiring quotes, or say your affirmations. Everything is going to be okay. Your hope will return, and I promise you that you will rediscover your joy once more.

ABOUT THE AUTHOR

Jenna is a wife, dog mommy, lifestyle blogger and entrepreneur. She empowers women to live a life of less worry, to rediscover their hopes and joys and to live a more heart-centered life. She resides in Minnesota with her husband Clinton and their two English Springer Spaniels Zoey and Lily.

Connect with her at www.jennaherrig.com

9

THE TRUTH ABOUT SUCCESS WITH RADICAL SELF-CARE

TOBI B FELDMAN

My cell phone is ringing. I feel my jaw clench, my teeth grind, and tension take over my entire body. I close my eyes, remind myself to breathe, and proceed to inhale deeply. Before exhaling, as I'm holding my breath, I remind myself that I can do this. I can handle this. Whatever "this" is on the other side of the ringing, I've got it.

Experience taught me that the sooner I picked up the call, the less time my mind had to inevitably wander to the catastrophic possibility that my child was no longer alive. More often than not the call didn't warrant the trauma I was enduring. I had just been so conditioned to stressful incoming calls about my son from my other children, my husband, the school—then the police, the courts, the case managers.

Roughly twelve years of traumatic responses like this held my body hostage to survival mode. Intellectually, I knew that my husband and I did all the right things, though it never felt like enough. My heart ached for connection, but my son had checked out. He was now physically gone from our home and had emotionally cut himself off from our family. I was broken and living in chronic physical and emotional pain.

I made the choice when my children were young to put my career as a speech-language pathologist on pause. I had decided to be home and focus on homeschooling all three of my children. My husband had become sick with a rare autoimmune disease and was on disability, and it was time for me to figure out going back to work. One child had gone off to middle school, and the oldest was the perfect age to be home with the youngest. I had continued my education, so I polished my skills to get up to date with technology and the changes in the field, got some fresh clothing and pulled out all my supplies. Felt much like a first day of school, full of excitement and trepidation!

What I hadn't counted on were the phone calls, the cycles of chaos and crisis, or the physical shut down my body endured. I persisted. I changed my hours, I shifted my days; I switched it all up and created an office in my home. At first, I tiptoed around my clients, and then I became more transparent with them about what was happening in my family. I had to cut back and ultimately shut down in order to be present to my family's needs and my physical and emotional wellbeing. At a gut level I knew it was the right thing to do, but it came with deep sadness and bitter resentment.

In retrospect, there are many situations I would have managed differently. As a parent I wanted to fix, heal, protect, and shield. As an empath, I took on all the emotions and energy without awareness. I turned my life inside out in the illusion that I could control what was unfolding in front of me. I thought being more available would help, and this may have been harmful to me, my relationships, and even to the families I'd served and was no longer working with.

I leapt back into an existing network marketing business. It was work that I could fit into the cracks of my life. It involved connecting with other adults and helping them with products that I had studied well. It was clearly my comfort zone. I knew the people, the company, and the potential, so I redefined my goals and forged ahead. Fortunately, there were also beneficial products for stress, anxiety, pain, and sleep because these were continuing themes in my life as the space between each crisis became smaller, and it became crystal clear that I was functioning more as full-time case manager than anything else.

Success for me was completely redefined by small wins of the human spirit as opposed to financial gains, titles, or ranks. I found myself damn proud to get out of bed on most days, to work out, or to engage in any form of self-care. I began to dig deep into my own emotions and release past traumas and negative baggage that were weighing me down and keeping me from moving ahead in my personal journey. I had connected with other women, all coming from their own journey, though all seeking emotional clearance, connection and the desire to shift the energy of what success meant.

Letting go of past "failures" was an essential piece of the journey. Releasing my perception that I had failed versus the reality of my circumstances and choices and giving myself permission to move into uncharted territory was a bit of success.

Once the shackles of failure were removed, I felt free to explore and delve into the heart of what fed my soul. Clarity took time, and the lens required constant tweaking, but I instantly knew when the ideas popped up that they were keepers. I liken the process to a masterpiece in the making, a lump of clay that keeps being wetted down and reshaped until it becomes a vessel of beauty and purpose.

Throughout my journey I had love and support from friends and family, and I had resources in the community locally as well as on a national/global scale. My husband and I worked diligently with a therapist through it all. We went seeking help with parenting issues, and then this search extended into all our areas of our family life, our relationship and ourselves. I credit it for the survival of our marriage! And yet what I longed for the most was women that truly "got it," that had been through similar fires. With them few words were needed to explain the minutia of the systems and processes or the depth of despair when the phone rang. Women that could teach me how to reclaim the life I had put on the back burner in a delusional effort to "save" my child. I worked with a dear friend that guided me back to myself, to loving myself again, to honoring the sacred space I required to heal. And another that invited me to imagine the unimaginable and manifest the possibility of a renewed relationship with my then estranged child.

The personal development journey I embarked upon opened doors to infinite possibilities, and I began to dream again, to set intentions and goals, to seek balance and peace, and to redefine boundaries and relationships. And this is where the success blossomed, in the spaces of possibility, of imagination and dreams. Dreams shaped into goals whittled into actions that brought me one baby step at a time closer to how I defined myself in the framework of success.

Now I am that woman for other women. I am the one who "gets it," and words don't need to be spoken. I see past the words and into the broken hearts and lost dreams. I understand the space occupied by unspeakable fear and the illusion that we can control any of what is happening. I stand firm in knowing that it all begins with the mamas, doing the deep work to let go of generational trauma, to change the stories, and to move beyond them. I am passionate about sustainable, radical self-care and unshakable self-love so that we thrive and model it for our families.

Becoming this woman for other women is my definition of success. It propels me out of bed in the morning and is the warmth in my heart as I lie down at night. I'm inspired daily with new ideas and opportunities to serve, support, and love. Recently, my child shared that he had no regrets about the experiences of the past, that they formed who he is today and were all part of his journey. Hearing that soothed my heart; it allowed me to acknowledge the wisdom of his words and further embrace my own journey. Success is a profoundly personal definition, and one that can't be judged from the outside looking in. We are each on our own mission and set our own course. We are the only ones who can declare when we have achieved success as we define it.

Financial abundance, the commonly defined measure of success, is also highly variable. A surplus of money may have been helpful in securing more resources or created less stress, but I don't believe it would have changed the trajectory of events. Financial success doesn't heal trauma, or repair relationships, nor does it guarantee safety or joy. I believe succeeding financially is a significant piece of the puzzle, for it's the fuel igniting us, freeing us to go forth, follow our hearts, our passions, and succeed as we ourselves define it.

And that said, when we tune in, listen, and follow our paths...abundance finds us in the richest of ways.

ABOUT THE AUTHOR

Tobi B Feldman, "the resilientAF midlife mama" is an eccentric entrepreneur. She's a Speech-Language Pathologist, Life Balance Coach, Author, Speaker, and Podcaster.

She successfully transformed her life from a chronically stressed, fibromyalgia-ridden, traumatized mama dealing with cycles of chaos and crisis in her family to being resilientAF with firmer boundaries, tighter relationships, and inner peace.

Female empowerment turns her on! She is passionate about supporting other women in reclaiming their own lives while in the throws of raising teens and young adults. She geeks out to the inner workings of the brain and how it affects getting S%&T done and how that impacts mental health.

Tobi lives amongst the waterfalls in Ithaca, NY with her husband, the youngest of her three kids, and her goofy Goldendoodle.

Connect with her at: http://gratefulmom.com

10

THE TRUTH ABOUT SUCCESS AFTER REJECTION

CYNTHIA MAE

"You can't come back here if you don't agree to believe what we believe right now," said a youth pastor and his wife to a thirteen-year-old girl, having pulled her into a study while the other teens played hide-n-seek during a youth lock-in night in the church.

That night I left my friends crying, wondering what had happened.

Going home wasn't my favorite thing, and I was always trying to find somewhere else to go. My mother, a recovered alcoholic, was essentially a single mother of four while my dads were never around. One father left when I was very young, and I only saw him on holidays at my grandparents'. The other was consumed by his life online. He was around, but not in the way I desperately needed. I had no structure. No guidance. When someone tried to guide me, I rebelled.

High school was my home. I was on every sports team, club, or program you could think of, and I fundraised ninety percent of my required costs for those teams. I was also a good student. I maintained a 4.0 GPA and was the best sharpshooter in the state, so I had teachers rooting for me.

My godparents' family was my saving grace. They are still one of the most constant, steadfast pieces of my ever-shifting life puzzle. They supported, guided, led and sheltered me when my parents didn't. Still, I rebelled often.

I needed guidance and a strong arm, but I didn't want it. What teenager wants to be told how to live, especially when she had been managing her high school career just fine?

Now, back to the church crisis. What happened? Seriously, I was thirteen. I had some questions previously brought up about a chapter in the Bible, and now all of a sudden I can't play with everyone else until I submit to certain beliefs? I was literally kicked to the curb with my overnight bag and told I couldn't stay.

Moving forward, I joined another church I knew from our church's summer softball leagues. I had great fun with this group, grew and learned a lot. I still talk to the youth pastor today.

Once I graduated high school—as salutatorian, even—I left for college and moved to the young adult's church group. I was a freshman living on campus, struggling with all-night study sessions, maintaining a 3.89 GPA at a private university on a scholarship. So many of my peers were there on their parents' dime and had grown up in private school, but it was a level that I struggled to keep up with. It was tough.

One Sunday evening that spring semester, I received an email from the wife of our church group leader. It said: "You're being a bad Christian woman by not making the effort to come to church."

Seventeen-year-old me said, "Fine," and never looked back.

In the summer of 2006, my high school boyfriend had been keeping it cozy in Germany with another lover, and in the fall my university's finance department was audited. The paperwork for my scholarship had been lost in the shuffle, and I had to pay $10,000, or I couldn't return in the spring.

YIKES.

I did what I knew and looked for something I could lean on. What I found was the military. I'd gone through three years of Junior Reserve Officers Training Corps in high school, so I felt I could handle this. I went and talked to a recruiter in January 2007. I left that same month for basic training. Gone. Bye, Felicia. My hometown and family were in the rear-view mirror as I left to start over.

My years in the military started to fly by. Deployment after deployment, boyfriend after boyfriend, and church was the last thing on my mind. Three deployments and two home stations later, finally about to jump ship in 2012 from my time as an active-duty photojournalist, I met the first man I wanted to marry.

He treated me great; it was like a fairy tale. But remember, I was rebellious, so the setting wasn't perfect. He was married but separated and getting a divorce. That should have been my first sign. We got married and spent our entire first year apart as he was sent to New York with the army and I was settling in Alaska. That year was rough, especially since my relationship with his previous wife wasn't the greatest and we shared the kids. Within the first year of discovering all the lies, pain and broken promises, I wanted a divorce. I felt trapped in the marriage for almost five years. Don't get me wrong: He had his great qualities, but we were toxic together. He never pulled through with therapy, and he turned the church against me.

Yes, I had tried church again. It was a unique situation—it was a fellowship program for military members at the house of a host. I had a lot of really great friends and strong bonds from this group.

All of those bonds shattered when I made a mistake. I was forcefully kicked out of the church group that I had frequented for seven years. The leader of that group's wife told everyone what I had done after my husband went to them in confidence, looking for guidance. No one came to me. Rumors spread, and I was handed a letter of banishment from my "military church family." Others involved in the mistake were still welcomed. My faith in family, trust, support and a home ceased to exist at this point.

I, sulking and wanting someone to love me and care about me, did find another man who seemed mature, but that failed. He lived with me for six months before I found out he was married.

A single mother at this point, I was broken. I had recently started a new job where I wasn't heard; I was ignored, but I kept it going to pay the bills even though I was miserable. My daughter was so happy, she just loved me so much. Then, all of a sudden, a shift happened.

I was given multiple travel assignments spread out over six months. I had no family in Alaska, so I reached out to see if my family could allow my daughter to stay with them while I completed my mission requirements. This was the bittersweet moment, you know. I did miss my daughter and had her traveling a lot as a young child, but my family received an extreme amount of quality time with her that wouldn't have been possible otherwise.

I don't care how many people told me that I was a bad mother. How could I let my daughter go while I was in Alaska for chunks of that time, hiking and having fun?

Easy. I knew my daughter was safe, and I had a job to do.

When I wasn't working, having my alone time was the BIGGEST, most beneficial self-care I had given myself in a long time. I rediscovered myself. I learned to love myself again. I went on dates; I went on hikes. And I found confidence again. I was in the best shape of my life, post childbirth.

That same summer, I found the love of my life, who adopted

my little girl. I am now one of the civilian leaders managing a billion-dollar military project and have one hell of a resume to back me up. I have two beautiful daughters and another one on the way. The self-care also offered me time to find Christ in the way that He needed me to hear Him—separate from painful church experiences. Every day I have my own time with Him on my hour-long drive to work. I get to feel it through the love of my children and family. We have never been closer.

This isn't my end game.

I discovered a lady who believes in me more than anyone, who has pushed and guided me into becoming my own leader. Sometimes what we need is a good, healthy mentor. I did a lot of surviving and maturing on my journey, and now I am ready to give back from my lessons learned.

Finally, I can go beyond for other people. I love mentoring others in how not to fail at being an adult and how to overcome the circumstances that life throws at them. Getting Back to Basics is a system I am creating based on my life's journey, when I tried to attack everything on my own. My past is influencing my present to help others grow from surviving hardship. I am learning to use my lessons to help guide others who have experienced a life of setbacks, failures and rejection.

Life shouldn't be this hard. Adulting shouldn't be this hard. Successful people aren't born successful or even with all the right tools and opportunities.

How would you overcome a lifetime of rejection? Sometimes, taking a shred of someone else's advice might just be that push you've always needed. A college professor said a phrase I'll never forget, which I will leave you with:

"Don't be so prideful to not let someone else serve you, for you then rob them of the opportunity to serve as well."

ABOUT THE AUTHOR

Cynthia is a Wife, Momma, Combat Veteran, Oiler, Coach, & Program Developer for Successful Adults. She empowers others to lean on each other for support, friendship and mentorship. She teaches that self-care is amongst the most important foundations to finding success. She has over 10 years of administrative skills that she also coaches and teaches others how to be successful in the workplace. She believes that getting to the life that you want to live shouldn't be hindered by how to buy a house, fears of having children, or not knowing what to do when something mechanical goes wrong. The Life UnsTRUctuReD Project is a program Cynthia is creating for others to share and discover the "lessons learned" about the trials and successes of becoming an adult, student, leader and employee in today's world. Connect with her at helloCynthiaMae.com

III

TENACITY & STRENGTH

11

THE TRUTH ABOUT SUCCESSFULLY THRIVING AFTER TRAUMA

ANGELA NEWHOUSE

TRIGGER ALERT – *This chapter deals with childhood sexual abuse and intense domestic violence.*

From a very young age I have had to be a fighter. I have had to don a suit of armor to protect myself from the trauma that just kept on coming. That armor turned into anger, resentment, isolation, and despair of ever being pain-free mentally and physically. As the armor hardened to stone, it grew bigger and bigger until it felt as though it surrounded me completely. I myself had turned into solid stone.

It literally felt like someone had stuck an IV of concrete into my arm and my body had now turned on me too. All the traumas I had endured, and the stress I had battled now transformed into medical issues. I was fighting a demon within my body that was torturing me just like the memories of the abuse.

I will never forget the first time I was betrayed by a loved one. I was seven. I was in my room and asked for help with my homework, and in he came. I was lying on the top bunk, propped up against some pillows. As I asked him how to solve a math problem, I felt his hand slide underneath my loose pajama shirt. I froze. What was he doing? I knew it was wrong immediately, but I did not know what to do. Then he started rubbing my nipple. I remember squeezing my arm tight against his and trying to shove his hand down and back out of my shirt, but he was persistent. During that moment I stopped talking, and as he pushed up against my arm and kept rubbing my nipple, he said, "Continue explaining the problem."

I will never forget how in one small moment my world would forever be changed. In that moment and many other moments to come, he broke my spirit and stripped away my self-worth. He escalated to rubbing between my legs and tortured me mentally and physically for years. He was so sly and devious—sometimes doing it quickly as my mother walked out of the room or rubbing on me at night when I was required to say goodnight and he would graze the areas and smile. I felt so icky in those moments and knew it was wrong, but he was the authority figure in the house so who would I tell and who would believe me?

As the years went on, I started learning what anger and hate were, and I knew without a doubt that I hated him. I started getting angry with those around me. Did they not know? Could they not see my pain? Maybe they knew but weren't going to stop it. I started pulling away from other male family members just because I had no trust in them at all, and I feared it would happen with them too. He stole my innocence as well as my ability to trust. I didn't know what to think anymore. What was right? What was wrong?

Way too often, people that don't get the help they need after childhood trauma fall victim to abuse in adulthood mostly because of a lack of confidence in themselves. I was that person. I met a narcissist when I was just eighteen years old. I was still carrying the scars from my childhood when I was first abused by him. Narcissistic abuse begins slowly and increases after each time that the narcissist gets away with it, in a similar way to the abuse of a child. Before you know it, you are being stripped of your self-worth, your mind and your freedom all over again.

I will never forget the moment when I did not feel free anymore. He had the control to give me life or take it away. Once, when I was at home and he was at the bar drinking with friends, my gut told me that it was going to be a bad night. It was a night that changed my life forever.

He had always had guns around and made verbal threats to use them, although up to that point he had never actually done it. There was something in the air that night, and a darkness I felt in my core that told me to think about what might happen if he did. I went into our spare room, where I knew the guns were, and I hid every bullet I could find. Then I crawled into bed clothed in case I needed to escape. That was the decision that set him off.

He came home and I could hear him stumbling through the kitchen, but I could tell by the way he walked that he was on a mission. As the bedroom door opened, a breeze wafted in, filled with the smell of alcohol. I pretended to be asleep, but I could hear that this was angering him. Right then he ripped the covers off me and his eyes went from brown to dark black. He saw that I was dressed, and I normally wasn't. He started yelling about things, and I tried to convince him that I was just cold and that was why I was dressed. He was in a rage. He said to me, "Well, if you are going to leave, then it will be in a pine box." He went to the spare room and got his pistol, and he walked back down the hallway towards me as I pleaded with him and tried to calm him. He wasn't having it.

In that moment terror struck my very core. The pistol he grabbed did not have the clip in it and as he went to put it in, I begged him to stop and reached up to grab it, but it was too late. I jumped as I heard the click of the gun. That is a moment that will haunt me for the rest of my life. He did it; he actually pulled the trigger. I will never know what possessed me to go and hide the bullets that night, but I believe it was a higher power telling me that I was not finished living, and that I had a purpose here even if I did not know it yet.

I am a big believer in the words NEVER GIVE UP. To me they are not just words but a lifestyle.

So many times during the moments of trauma we jump to the conclusion that we are the unworthy ones, the broken ones, and the damaged ones. In reality, we didn't ask for this trauma to be inflicted upon us. The abuser is the damaged and broken one. We need to change our mindset from thinking that we have imperfections or are unworthy of happiness because of trauma that was inflicted upon us. Society views us as "having issues." I view us as having strength, perseverance, and the will to survive.

We need to stand tall and yell from the mountain tops that "I AM A SURVIVOR AND I AM WORTHY OF GREATNESS!"

You need to know that you are worthy of whatever life you dream up. What you have been through has given you the tough skin to handle anything thrown your way. I spent way too many years thinking that I was flawed or that there was something about me that just attracted pain and trauma. All I needed was a change of mindset to find my self-worth, and that black cloud that was sprinkling drops of trauma over my life started to break and sunshine began to cover me like a blanket of hope.

Along our journey to survive, we harden in a way very few understand. Everyone can make bad decisions, but we sometimes make a few more. What we need to remember is that the bad decisions do not have to be a life sentence. Life traumas and bad decisions that we hold on to are like a broken wing: You will never be able to fly until you fix it.

Whether your scars are visible or deep inside of you, they are a reminder that you are a survivor. Some people view their scars as ugly, as broken pieces of themselves that can never be fixed, and they consider themselves damaged. While I understand the dark place that we go to, because I have been there, that is no place to stay. You may have one defining moment in your life where you just felt like you could not go on. I have had many. I started to get numb and started to think that my life was just meant for destruction. The key word there is "think."

The key to being able to view your scars as beautiful has to do with:

*Mindset
*Determination to survive
*Faith in a higher power
*Finding your purpose

Look at the mindset transformation examples below.

Child abuse: The child feels flawed and attracting or deserving of the abuse. In a perfect world, we would teach our children to know that when abuse happens it is not their fault. They are not flawed or broken—the abuser is. Mindset needs to be taught and instilled in our children from as young as possible to help them mentally tackle the situation and hopefully long before they turn the blame on themselves. They are not flawed and should not feel so.

We all have a purpose; we just need the clouds to part and the sun to shine on our souls to light the fire that we know is inside of us. I have created some tools to help you on your journey and wish you the very best in healing your wounds, using your scars as steppingstones and taking your mindset from broken to survivor and from a bad decision maker to a wiser one.

Take the time to change your mindset, find your self-worth and build your confidence so that you can follow your dreams. Have you even dreamed lately? I never knew that was possible until I started healing. I did not think I was allowed to dream. I thought it was childish, and that I needed to focus on surviving and sustaining a life mending my broken pieces. I believed that dreaming was just a waste of time and getting my hopes up for nothing. I was wrong.

Dreams can light a fire deep inside us that we never knew was there. Following your dreams can turn your life into a new reality that you never knew was possible. There is no reason for your trauma to stop you from accomplishing your dreams. If you need help getting a plan together, then that is what I am here for. I can help coach you into a new mindset full of worthiness, of hope for a brighter future, and help you build your confidence to chase those dreams and change your life for the better!

ABOUT THE AUTHOR

Angela Newhouse is a survivor of multiple life traumas and maintains a never give up mindset. She is strong willed and determined to be livin' a happy life no matter what roadblocks life presents. She believes in being driven by your heart and always promotes positivity over negativity. As someone who has been through many difficult life challenges, she is using her experience and knowledge to help others overcome their own struggles. She is helping others to never give up on life, giving them the tools to help them through tough situations and teaching them to see the brighter side of things. Sunshine is one of Angela's favorite things, she says it warms your heart in ways that are indescribable and she wants to be the sunshine in your life during your moments of darkness.

Connect with her at AngelaNewhouse.com

12

THE TRUTH ABOUT SUCCESS IN PURSUING YOUR DREAMS RELENTLESSLY

DEBBIE ROTHE

I did not realize when I got dressed that morning that the baby kicking inside me would someday be bragging to her friends and teachers about the journey I was embarking on. A decision unlocking a life of unimagined possibility was about to be made. But first, I had to make it through this three-hour graduation ceremony.

I shifted uncomfortably on the metal seat as I watched my husband's graduation ceremony at Central Michigan University. Unable to get relief for my aching back, I stood up and walked stiffly to a side railing out of the way from other spectators. Blaise made a summersault in my belly. Christmas was approaching, and it was only three months until she would be born. I guess we were both excited her dad was graduating with his master's degree in Education. Henry had taken classes in the evenings and weekends while teaching full time. That had meant late nights, getting home after dinnertime, weekend homework and less time for us together. I was happy to see it coming to an end as he walked across the stage to get his diploma.

The speeches were of the typical motivating nature about succeeding against the odds, pursuing your dreams, and changing the world. All of these sentiments resonated deeply with me and started a fire inside that was not just pregnancy heartburn. I had always told myself after I graduated with my bachelor's degree, six years prior, that I would go back to school and get an advanced degree. I wanted more from my life. I loved learning and growing. I worried about being stuck and not having options because I lacked the education. I feared being underestimated and pigeon-holed in a dead-end career because I "only had a four-year degree." The only reason why I had not done it yet was that I couldn't see it happening. I wasn't sure how to do it. Watching Henry graduate helped me envision it, and for the first time I felt it could happen.

Blaise kicked me like a punching bag while the list of graduates was read, and my mind drifted to how I would earn my Ph.D. *Where do I begin? Is it possible?* It felt a bit surreal that I was entertaining this notion right before a major life event. As we drove home, I told Henry what I was thinking, and he was immediately supportive. I could see the result in my mind, but I wasn't sure what the path looked like yet. It was time to do my homework.

I decided to start with a couple of trusted mentors at work, where I was met with two completely opposite responses. The first person was incredibly supportive. They told me it was possible; others had done it and I could do it all while working. That was an important factor. I needed to keep my day job. The second individual tried to be kind but stifled a laugh, staring at my second-trimester silhouette. This person sighed and very gently said, "That's nice, but you are going to be a mom now..." The voice trailed off and I do not remember what was said next. Doubt filled my head, and I realized: *They think this is ridiculous; that I am ridiculous. How dare I want more?* After essentially being patted on the head, I left the office feeling deflated.

As I am persistent, I sought advice from others. And so it went on like a tennis match, back and forth. From "Great idea! Let's make it happen" to "You are doing what?" It was confusing and frustrating. The swing from supportive to creating more barriers had me thinking it was impossible. But I just couldn't let it go. It was MY DREAM, not theirs. They couldn't begin to understand what this meant for me as a woman, a mom-to-be of a daughter, a scientist, and a dreamer.

After days of conflicting advice, I vented to my husband about how scared and frustrated I was. I wanted to do it but wasn't sure how, especially after so many people had tried to talk me out of it. I was full of doubt about how I could make it all happen with my day job and becoming a mother. I remember blurting out, "I just don't know if I can do it!"

That is when he paused, turned to me, and asked, "When have you ever not been able to do something?"

I was quiet for a long time. I was unable to recall not being able to do something once I had decided that I was, in fact, going to do it. He then went on to say, "I can't believe you would even consider for a minute not doing it."

There it was. Affirmation from someone who knew me better than anyone else. Support from the person who was going to be on the journey with me. My resolve hardened. I knew I had to do it, or I would regret it forever. I was ready to make it happen.

With the decision behind me, I was ready to get started. It was time to...wait. I thought I needed to wait. I did wait until Blaise was born, and then thought I needed to wait until I had another baby. And wait until I came back to work, got my feet under me and could then GO! In the meantime, I had a conversation with a close friend who helped me find a university with a distance-education program offering the degree I wanted in Material Science. She helped me make the connection with the faculty and start the process.

I met with the professor who would be my advisor and told

him my plans. It was the summer of 2007, and I was looking at starting in the fall of 2008. That timeframe would give me a chance to have a second baby, get back to work and then start the Ph.D. program. I did not share the baby part with him. I needed to take the GRE in the fall, and that would give me plenty of time.

He had a different perspective, suggesting, "Why don't you start in spring of 2008? Get started taking courses even if the application has not been approved. You can then transfer those credits to your program."

I hesitated with my response, not wanting to tell him what I was thinking. I wished to blurt out, "I want to have another baby, and everyone will look at me like I am a big joke if I go back to school while pregnant! I can't do that!" Instead, I replied, "Umm. Okay." All the while cringing and imagining being massively pregnant and sweating profusely as I gave a presentation to a class of college students. Great! *They'll think I am a joke and don't belong there.* I had locked on to that vision and struggled to let it go.

I shared how I felt about being "the pregnant grad student" with a dear colleague. She assured me that people loved to see women doing this, and it made her smile when she saw pregnant women giving talks and not showing shame. The fear was so powerful because of how I had been treated when I'd broached the subject with certain people I trusted and thought would be supportive. It is amazing how fear and judgement can overwhelm us and stop us from pursuing what we care about. The biggest triumph is silencing those voices and proving them wrong. That is exactly what I did.

I started classes in the spring of 2008 like my advisor had hoped. It was a lot of work, but I made it work. For my end-of-semester presentation, I shared research I had done with holographic optical tweezers, a technology that imparts momentum on a microscopic particle by focusing a laser. That means you can move the particle with light; something you might expect to see in a sci-fi movie. The reaction from my professor and fellow grad students had this mom from the Midwest feeling less like a joke and more like a superstar. I ended the semester with all As and a positive pregnancy test.

I was due to have Cadence in January of 2009. It meant a hot, sweaty trip to New Mexico in the summer to meet with faculty and tour the campus. I registered for more courses in the fall and had a good start on my research, which I presented just before Christmas. After having a healthy, happy baby, I went on maternity leave. During my twelve weeks off, I met weekly with my local advisor at a coffee shop to do a directed study on polymer membranes for lithium-ion battery applications. I continued my regular courses once back from maternity leave. It was a blur but went something like this:

Write a research paper on electrolytic lenses. Study. Saturday morning experiments in the lab. Put kids to bed. Late nights doing homework. More writing. Trips to New Mexico to present research proposals, meet with faculty and accept academic achievement awards for having the highest GPA in the Materials Department.

Yes, a thirty-something mom working full time at a Fortune 100 company did this. That was me.

There were times I wanted to quit. It. Was. HARD! There were days I wondered how I was ever going to have the strength to continue. The negative voices around me continued. When people found out what I was doing, the reaction was like before. I was met with either admiration or admonishment for how crazy it was, along with being told my research was not good enough and not a real Ph.D. I could not have done it without my husband's love and support, encouragement from friends, mentors, advisors, and family coming over to babysit.

After seven years of homework, writing papers, Saturdays at the lab doing research, sweat, tears, frustration, two babies, and late nights collecting small angle x-ray scattering data from the advanced photon light source at Argonne National Laboratory, I had created a piece of work I was proud of. On Mother's Day weekend, May 8, 2015, with my husband and my six- and nine-year-old daughters, I walked across the stage in Socorro, New Mexico to get my diploma. A well-deserved, fought for and earned Ph.D. I did it. The feeling was sweet, and the memory is even sweeter.

In my dissertation I wrote this dedication: "To my two favorite people that inspired this journey. Blaise and Cadence, relentlessly pursue your dreams with all your heart. Continuously seek knowledge, striving to leave this world a better place than you first found it, ensuring a future filled with abundance and joy. May you always have clean water. To Henry, this dream would not have been realized without your love and support. I look forward to our next adventure."

And here we go...

ABOUT THE AUTHOR

Dr. Debbie Rothe is an adoptee, coach, mom, wife, business owner and global leader at a Fortune 100 company. Debbie is passionate about inspiring possibility and unlocking achievement so that together we can light up the universe. It is her mission to be an unwavering force of positivity in this world. She founded her company, Winspire Coaching & Consulting during a global pandemic with a vision of helping people who are exhausted trying to prove themselves to create a life where they are powerful and thriving. Debbie's teams experience higher resiliency to stress, and high employee satisfaction. She champions inclusion, collaboration, & values the diverse perspectives from her people. She lives in Michigan with her husband, Henry and daughters, Blaise and Cadence. Connect with her at http://www.winspirecoaching.com

13

THE TRUTH ABOUT SUCCESSFULLY REINVENTING YOURSELF AFTER FIFTY

RACHEL KUEHN

"There is freedom waiting for you,
On the breezes of the sky,
And you ask "What if I fall?"
Oh but my darling,
What if you fly?"
— Erin Hanson

I sat sobbing on the couch, with my husband looking at me not knowing what to do or say. I was inconsolable. I am not usually someone who cries, but I was unable to hold back these feelings and tears anymore. I was at my breaking point, living on the "hamster wheel" and not being able to figure out how to get off. I felt stuck, trapped, hopeless, and unable to even think of a way out of my current situation. You hear people talk about seeing the light at the end of the tunnel when things are starting to get better, but if we're being honest, I could barely see the opening of the tunnel, let alone any light. I knew something in my life needed to change and fast.

My work as a hospice nurse, managing a caseload of thirteen to twenty people and their families, was rewarding and purposeful, but it left me burned out, with nothing left to give to my family or myself. The work was time-intensive, with all the charting and other parts of the job requiring me to work several hours of overtime every night just to keep up.

The stress was starting to take a toll on my health, and I appeared to be developing autoimmune-like symptoms which made it even harder to meet the demands of my busy work schedule due to fatigue. I was spending more time at work and less time with my family, which made things even more stress-ful. On top of that, hospice work was a daily reminder of how I should be living my life. Supporting people during their end-of-life journey made it impossible to ignore the fact that I was letting my own life pass me by. I felt like I was treading above water, paddling like crazy just to stay afloat—only to get up the next day and do the same thing all over again, year after year.

You might wonder what kept me living that way for so long, unsatisfied with my groundhog-day life. The truth was, I couldn't see a way out. I was trapped. I had health insurance and did not think that I could afford to lose my income. I also did not even know where to start. When my health started to be affected, it was a big a-ha moment for me. At this point, I knew I could not afford to stay in my current situation, or I might not physically be here until retirement. I asked myself what kind of life I was living. What if I was told I would die in the next six months: What would I do differently? Living a life "of not living" was not on that list. If you were asked that question, what would you do differently in your life?

The day I hit my breaking point, I knew I couldn't keep working at this pace, meeting the demands of my employer and the needs of the families in my care. Whenever I or other co-workers mentioned that the workload was too much, we were usually met with a response such as, "You have to change your mindset," or "No one else is reporting these issues," or "You must have a time-management problem." I found this very disheartening, and it made me feel like I was the one with the problem even though others were saying and feeling similar issues.

As more responsibility fell on the case managers and less help was available to us, I knew something in my life needed to change. I struggled with the realization that my identity was completely tied to my job title and role. I knew it was crazy, but my brain was telling me, "You're not a nurse unless you are taking care of people at the bedside," even though I knew that was not true. I struggled between knowing that I had worked so hard to get where I was and feeling as though I had lost all of my creativity and didn't know how to have fun anymore. I had lost my inspiration and forgotten how to dream.

I had to take a hard look at my life and the direction it was heading in. I knew my work was meaningful, but if I wanted to get everything done and be on time, then it required me to have short visits with my patients. Taking care of my patients was the reason I chose the nursing profession, not the charting and bureaucratic regulations. I realized then I needed to reinvent myself and come up with a plan. I found that I was holding myself back—feeling limited and trapped. I was thinking small when I wanted to play big. I desired to show up in a way that would allow me to make a huge impact on the world, not just through one person at a time. At that moment I didn't even know what that meant, but I felt it inside.

I slowly started to dream again. I tried to identify what was stopping me from going after my dreams of helping others in a big way. What did I fear most about leaving my job? Was it that I wouldn't be able to afford it? Was I worried about what others would think? I questioned whether I could make it financially or not. These were hard questions, and I knew that if I had to continue living that way, I would begin to wonder whether my life was even worth living. It was then that I decided I needed to change. I needed to follow my dreams, and I decided that I would find a way.

First, I needed to stop making excuses. I started dreaming of different jobs that I could do and began designing a plan for the life I wanted to live. It was time to stop wishing for change and start taking action steps to move me in the direction of a better life.

I got intentional with my life. I journaled ideas, identified what inspired me and what brought me joy. In my fifties, I started designing the life I had always wanted. You're never too old to make a change!

It is scary stepping out and doing something new, but it is exciting too. I have found that I'm able to dream again, and that creative and inspiring thoughts excite me like they used to. It had been so long since I had those feelings, I almost did not recognize them. I did not realize the toll that my job had been taking on my entire body, mind, and spirit.

I started setting small goals at first, creating a plan to still bring in an income so that I could afford my responsibilities while leaving my current job. I did have to get creative and do some jobs short-term until I could afford to get to the place where I did not need that level of income. The other thing I learned was not to overthink new plans and just jump in. I was consistent in my actions, working toward my new dreams and goals.

Are you living your life with purpose and joy? Sharing what you are passionate about? Are you working in a job that gets you excited? Does it allow you to live life? It is never too late to reinvent yourself. When you find the place you are meant to be in, you will know it. It will spur you to dream bigger, scare you a little, and excite you all at the same time. This is the spark that will set you on fire!

One of the things I would highly recommend is to take the Gallup CliftonStrengths test. This test will give you your Top 5 strengths for under twenty dollars. Rhonda Boyle's website has a great blog with videos explaining the strengths and how they work in your life. This was a powerful assessment. Learning my Top 5 strengths and how they worked in my life helped me realize who I am authentically so I could focus on my strengths and not my weaknesses. So often we look at our weaknesses and try to improve on those. But when I found out what my strengths were, I realized that it is more important to focus on the things I am good at rather than trying to change who I am. For the first time in a long time, learning these results gave me "permission" to be myself instead of who others wanted me to be. When I was younger, people made fun of me for being my authentic self. I found myself going more inward, just wanting to blend in like a wallflower for most of my life. After taking the assessment, I realized exactly why I was the way I was. It was empowering. Not everyone will want you to be you, but to fly you must get to the place of accepting yourself and willing to take the risk.

At this point, I was ready to move forward. I left my job as a case manager hospice nurse and leapt. The first leap is scary but liberating at the same time. I found when I was finally at the place where I was no longer letting my identity be dictated by my career and no longer allowing my situation to control me and my thoughts, that everything I had been worrying about kept me stuck in my situation. Once I left my job, I realized that I was not as stuck as I had thought. I know it's hard to believe, but when you feel trapped, you are so exhausted trying to get through the day that you can't see beyond it. There is little inspiration, joy, or happiness when you are living in this manner.

So, what if you just design your dream life, leap, and trust?

Like the quote above says, "But what if you fly?" I've been there; I leapt into the great unknown. I got to a place where I knew I had to follow my dreams. Not everyone understood or supported me, but it didn't matter. That leap was the most freeing feeling I have ever experienced. I understood then that I had kept myself trapped and stuck, believing that I could not do something different or reinvent myself. I told myself that I had to work to pay my bills, have health insurance, and the other list of excuses I gave myself. Yes, those things are important, and I do have to own up to my responsibilities. This was where I had gotten stuck. I was exhausted working a job that required more of me than I was getting paid for both monetarily and in time. I wasn't thinking outside the box, dreaming of other ways that I could still earn money while doing something I loved. I was stuck, not experiencing life in a meaningful way.

I jumped, but I didn't fall and hit the ground. It was surprising, freeing, enlightening, and not at all scary. I saw things from a perspective that I had not had before. A huge weight was lifted off my shoulders. I saw opportunities and started feeling creative again. These feelings had been missing from my life for years. I never did fall like I thought I would in all the stories I had created in my head. It was the exact opposite: I soared and realized that I was unlimited. I wrote the book I had been dreaming about and marveled at how many lives I could touch with one book versus one person at a time.

Do not be afraid to dream big and take the leap. Are you ready to fly? Now is the time to start dreaming of the life you want to live. Create a plan and make your dreams come true. You are worth it!

ABOUT THE AUTHOR

Rachel Kuehn is a nurse, author, Reiki Master, speaker, entrepreneur, holistic health and hospice advocate. She is the never-ending advocate for taking care of YOU and living the life you were truly meant to live! Rachel is the author of "Confessions of a Hospice Nurse – the journey of life and death and the lessons in between."

Connect with her at www.rachel-kuehn.com

14

THE TRUTH ABOUT SUCCESSFULLY CHANGING YOUR MINDSET TO GAIN A PEACEFUL LIFE

GRETA OLECHNO

A ll my life I thought stress, chaos, and even trauma were normal ways of life. I truly believed that without them I would not accomplish anything. Stress was such a normal feeling for me that the less stress I experienced, the less normal I felt. I grew up thinking that stress was what keeps us alive.

Growing up in a poor, chaotic, communist Poland in the early 80s was not horrible, but it was not a way of life that sets you up for success. Yes, I do believe it shaped me in many ways, and for that I am grateful, but it also set me up for failure in almost everything I did in my life.

Moving to a new country and continent with no understanding of the language was stressful and traumatic. As a child, I eventually adapted and kept going. Witnessing my mom experience hardship amplified it that much more for me.

I eventually settled into my new life, but the stress never went away. It just got bigger and more complicated as I grew up. I would feel very uncomfortable if I was in a place where the atmosphere was calm and grounded, and I would go out of my way to seek out drama, chaos and stress as it made me feel "normal."

I went through life making choices based on how much stress I was experiencing—and the more stressed I was, the better I thought I felt. I did most things backwards and somehow always accomplished most of what I wanted, but in a complicated and weird way that today I know was not healthy for me and my spirit. I was basically solving an easy task by taking multiple unnecessary steps.

After my short-lived nursing career in a very high-stress environment, I finally got the job of my dreams. It came with stress, of course, but I was okay with that because I had convinced myself that I worked best under stress.

I was a special education teacher working with medically fragile children, and it was the best job in the world. The children I worked with became my teachers over the years, and I began to understand how important and precious life really is.

Because I loved my job, I didn't see how stressful and toxic the environment had gotten over the years. I started to become blinded by the moral obligation I thought I had to help these children, and by doing that I was ignoring all the signs of burnout. I was working non-stop, and at home I was strenuously defending my reasons for working instead of spending time with my family. I was short-tempered and always too tired to do anything fun with my own kids. I also had a hobby that turned into a business, making aroma jewelry and macramé wall decor, which took over my weekends. I thought that I really enjoyed doing markets and expos on top of my already stressed, stretched life, and unconsciously justified the reasons for my hobbies.

I got to the point of no return where I couldn't sleep, was having panic attacks on Sunday nights, and felt like crawling into a hole and never coming out. My health declined, my weight soared, and everything else just went downhill from there.

After fifteen years of stretching myself thin, I ended up going on stress leave and feeling ashamed that I could not keep going, doing what I thought I loved doing. I felt like a failure.

I was in a dark hole that I had dug for myself over the years, and I did not see any way out.

I had many visits with my doctor, who suggested I start seeing a psychologist and after a while suggested antidepressants. That's when I finally lifted my head, looked at her and muttered, "There's got to be another way." I was not willing to go on antidepressants, at least not yet. I knew there had to be more that I could do, more that I had not tried, in order to crawl out of the darkness without prescription drugs.

The psychologist's sessions were great, because they allowed me to see the issue at hand and assess what I wanted from and for my life.

I decided to get back to my essential oils and supplements right away and began to explore self-help books that I had had for years on my bookshelf.

At this time, I stumbled upon a conference in my city where I met an amazing woman named Martha Krejci. Her presentations completely changed my mind about how I was going to get my life back to balance. I decided to change my mindset and dive into some of her courses, and they paved the way for me and helped me realize that I have a greater purpose.

I had always been a massive believer that mindset and mindfulness were essential, but I had never fully applied them to my everyday life. I could teach their importance to my students, but I was not using that knowledge for myself.

I began my new journey by being grateful for waking up every morning. I started to be thankful for the little things that before I had had no time to notice. As silly as it may sound, a simple little thing like a coffee in the morning was a way for me to be in the moment and appreciate the start of my day.

I started to be grateful for what I had and for my family. Especially my husband, who was my rock at my lowest; and he understood exactly how I felt, as he had gone through it himself two years before my breakdown. Things started to present themselves as opportunities, and I could see hope again.

I started to practice daily meditation, which helped me discover things about myself I didn't know were possible. I began to be more aware of my surroundings, and I felt like I was regenerating from a state of deep sleep and, at times, even a nightmare. I could not believe I had waited that long to see it all so clearly.

I began to do everything mindfully. I would go for walks, mindfully absorbing everything around me and enjoying it to the fullest. I did everything mindfully. It brought me to where I would begin to notice what I actually enjoyed and what I didn't. Finally, after a month of this, I decided that I would not be going back to work. I wrote my letter of resignation with a grateful heart. Even though work was what pushed me to my breaking point, I still hesitated to hand in my letter.

In hindsight, it was the most beautiful and liberating day ever. As I was driving home, the sun came out and was so intensely bright that I had to pull over and soak it all in.

I believe at that moment, God was smiling down on me as if He wanted me to know that for the first time in my life, I did something for me and me alone!

I had tears in my eyes, and I just kept saying *thank you* over and over again. I didn't worry about our finances, what the next step was going to be, or how I would make a living. All I thought about was how grateful I was to be in that moment.

I continue to add more little habits (good habits) to a routine that is now part of me, and I can't imagine my new life without them.

Here are a few:

Daily affirmations to remind myself that I am exactly as God created me and that I can do anything I set my mind to.

Daily meditation to help me uncover new skills I did not know I had.

Daily gratitude journal because it's a good reminder that there is always something to be grateful for.

Time blocking my to-do list so I stay on track and accomplish everything I set out to do.

Boundary setting for myself and others, which was a foreign thing to me before. I would say "yes" even though deep down I was screaming "no."

I stay motivated by taking on self-help courses and surrounding myself with supportive people because staying motivated requires avoiding naysayers and seeking out positive support.

Shaking off others' expectations and imitating beliefs is essential to living my most authentic and balanced life.

These steps are working for me, and they help me get what I want out of my own unique life.

And it all started with finding my true self.

ABOUT THE AUTHOR

Greta Olechno is a compassionate, intuitive advisor and life coach who empowers people to make confident choices and decisions in their lives.Through her journey of dealing with stress and unmanaged chaos, she has learned how to overcome the challenges that kept her back from having a balanced life. She is now following her soul and serving others by offering intuitive life coaching, guidance and creating a community for peer-to-peer support. She specializes in helping those who seek a holistic approach to recognizing and managing their lives impacted by toxic environments, stress and chaos. She supports her clients by allowing them to gain clarity to make aligned choices unique to their own inner calling.

Get in contact with her today to see how you can begin working together.

Connect with her at www.gretaolechno.com

15

THE TRUTH ABOUT SUCCESS AFTER MANY FAILURES

LYNN EADS

I stood in the kitchen with my heart pounding in my chest. It felt like the world had stopped turning and then restarted all at once. A wave of emotion came over me as I saw the determination on my mom's face. I knew she had made her decision, and that was the end of her marriage. I was eleven years old.

The divorce was emotional, as it is for all kids. I didn't want to be another statistic. I decided that I needed a plan for my life. I was determined be optimistic, persistent, and stay true to myself. I decided with a deep resolve that I would be a forever student of life and strive to figure things out independently. I wanted a way of life that was self-supporting, yet still included a happy marriage and children. I wanted financial freedom, and more importantly, time to spend with family. At that point in time, I set my future life goals. I didn't realize that the strong, influential women in my life had already laid a solid foundation for me.

I want women of any age to know that it's okay to use the word "failure." If you have failed in something, as I have, just know that it's okay. It happens to everyone, and I believe that we are all in this together. I have shifted, pivoted, and restarted many times over. I want to encourage you to never give up. What keeps me going are the women who have inspired me to continue growing throughout my life.

As a result, I want to inspire women to be driven, to better themselves and to learn from my mistakes and wisdom. Since young adulthood, I've tried many times to launch my own business, but almost all of them were not the right fit, or they flat out failed. That being said, I never gave up. I kept rolling forward, searching for the answers and the right business fit.

Before I got married, I was a working woman in the legal industry. After my children were born, I started thinking about things I could do to work from home. I opened a typing dictation service business for attorneys. One of the main things I learned working from home is that kids love to talk to you when you are on the phone! I had the chance to sharpen my solution skills; I bought a business phone that had an on-hold button. I also learned that I needed to do something more than typing. I didn't understand how to market the business, and it was before the age of the internet. I failed.

I was also intrigued by the MLM industry. I tried my luck over the years from selling books, to kitchen tools, to scrapbooking tools and even legal services. I discovered that I was spending more time away from home in the evenings and missing out precious time with my children. Also, in each case I wasn't guided or motivated to build the businesses. I was not making the money that I thought I would make. I did enjoy being an end user of the products, but in the end I failed.

Next, I purchased an existing business. I did it in the hopes that my husband would leave his career and join me. I made the decision to do this because I wanted to build a business so that we could achieve financial and time freedom for our growing family. I didn't write a business plan, forecast the business financials, or write a marketing plan. After investing over $90,000 and building it up for two years, I had to let it go. I learned some very valuable lessons about running a business as a woman in a predominantly male industry.

My husband was not onboard and felt he couldn't give up his career. After I had sold the customer base and liquidated all the equipment and assets, I still had to make payments on the payroll taxes for several years. I also learned that my strong suit was in sales, but not accounting. I have a "quick-start" style personality and my husband does not. This had a big impact on my decision to jump into a business without all the facts, thinking I could make it work. As a result, I failed.

In 2016, I began building my own personal brand, "Learn with Lynne." I continue setting good examples of motherhood, friendship, optimism, persistence, kindness and positive mindset through promoting my own brand with no reliance on anyone, anything or any company. Everything I've learned about these things I've learned from three influential women in my life: my mom, my aunt, and my grandma. They are all strong women in their own right, and the inspiration for my drive to success.

What I admire most about my mom is her resilience, bravery and her love and devotion for her children. She was a young mom who had her first child at age nineteen (me!). After her divorce, she made several sacrifices by going back to work as a waitress, giving up her social life and missing out on countless hours of being with her children. She worked hard to put food on the table and give us the best life possible. One of the biggest lessons I learned from her was how set a good example and overcome life's challenges. She taught me to always lead with my heart, put family first and to serve others. My mom is my hero.

Then came my aunt (my mother's sister). She was thirteen years old and I was two when she came to live with us. Tragically, her parents (my grandparents) had both passed away in the same year, just four months apart. She was really like a big sister to me, more than an aunt. I admire her courage and inner strength. She moved out when she was twenty-one, secured a job and an apartment. I was sad that she moved out, but happy for her that she achieved her goal of living on her own and supporting herself.

My maternal grandma was a seat frame worker at an assembly plant in Detroit, Michigan. She worked alongside men but was paid less. This was one of her biggest pet peeves. She was all for woman's equality. She was feisty and a genuine fire-cracker.

These strong women in my family have continued to inspire me. Some of the daily things they taught me and that keep me focused and productive are:

- Setting intentions for the day
- Checking in daily with my mindset
- Creating affirmations for my goals
- Drinking plenty of water
- Keeping a positive mental attitude

I hope you can use these tips to inspire YOU daily.

These past few years, I have been growing personally and so has my brand. This feels "right." I'm showing up, in my true authentic self. I have realized that in addition to helping parents raise their children as a nanny, I can expand my reach and offer coaching, courses and classes to thousands of families through online platforms. I believe I have found my true path to my personal business success.

Raising my children was the real highlight and crowning achievement of my life. I was determined to set good examples and teach them the skills they needed as adults. I believe I have taught them to be driven, resilient, strong adults by example. I succeeded.

Being a wife, parent, nanny, and businesswoman has made me more driven than ever. Yes, I have failed, but I am STILL driven. If you have failed, give yourself some grace and keep going. Stand up to keep your hopes and dreams alive. Every failure is an opportunity to learn. It's okay to say, "I failed." Just learn from the experience and pick yourself back up again.

ABOUT THE AUTHOR

Lynn is a native Michigan Author, Parenting Coach, Speaker, Mom, Wife, Grandma and Professional Nanny. She enjoys helping families raise their children through Parenting Coaching sessions, Parent Courses and Classes. She incorporates teachings through art, music reading, imagination, positivity and encouragement. She has over a dozen courses outlined on Parenting and other subjects that will begin rolling out in 2021! The first two "Power of Positive" and "Parenting Pre-Schoolers" will launch in the spring of 2021 on her website: http://learnwithlynne.com

In addition, she also has a custom diffuser jewelry line that established in 2017. She says that her inspiration comes from people she knows and meets. You can find her current inventory designs on her online shop: http://learnwithlynn.square.site

IV

FAMILY & COURAGE

16

THE TRUTH ABOUT SUCCESS IN MARRIAGE

ANNA STAGER

I lay in the dark, hot tears streaming down my face. Seven months of marriage had passed, and I longed to share my heart with my sleeping husband but struggled to do so. I thought marriage would feel different. I thought it would somehow magically wipe away my loneliness. Instead, I lay next to the man I loved feeling alone, like the only person in the world.

Ten years later, we sat across the table from each other. After years of infertility and a long adoption process, we were finally parents. Our hearts burst with love and yet we struggled to transition into our new role. Our baby was incredibly tiny, with special needs requiring constant care all day and all through the night. We felt weary emotionally and physically.

In addition to the toll of caring for our sweet son all night, I still worked a nightly transcription job. I felt certain I was doing more during the night than my husband. Much more.

What had happened to the "supporting each other" and "working together" we had learned during our first decade of marriage? Something had to change...and soon.

So, sitting across from Steve, I prepared for a verbal war. My chest tightened and I clenched my fists, ready to demand my needs get met.

On our wedding day, I had promised to love, support and sacrifice for Steve. Now my focus turned to my own wounds and needs. I let the circumstances confirm my deepest negative beliefs about myself...I was alone.

To be fair, my husband also felt exhausted and frustrated. Each was perfectly poised to push the other further away.

But in that conversation, something happened. Something surprising. Something good.

Instead of fighting we started seeing. Instead of demanding we started asking. Instead of hiding we started exposing. A shift was happening. We began to understand something about our problems, and something about the other person. How? We moved from sitting across the table to sitting on the same side— literally and emotionally.

What if the other person was not the problem, not the enemy? What if the real problem, the thing that divided us, wasn't a certain behavior, or making sure each person took equal shares of nighttime duty? What if the real problem was deeper, and simpler?

As we sat *together*, on the same side of the table, we began to see that the real problem was *in* us, each of us. You see, the real enemy was our own hardheartedness toward the other. It was the perspective that chose life as an individual, "alone and on my own against the world." Clearly, that path led to loneliness and anger.

There was only one true way forward... We had to choose **"Team."**

How'd we get *here*?

No one goes to their wedding day hoping their marriage will end in separation. People wholeheartedly commit themselves with beautiful vows. We all enter marriage with a genuine intention to love and a deep desire to be loved in return. As King Solomon said, "What a person desires is unfailing love." You see it in humans from the beginning: a baby reaching his arms for his mother, a toddler running to her grandpa in delight or children shouting out, "Mommy, watch me!"

We all long to be the couple enjoying a satisfying marriage. In the beginning we say, "Oh yes, I know we aren't perfect, but we will love each other, and it will be good!"

Then on the honeymoon or months after, our spouse hurts us deeply. It isn't just an annoyance easily brushed away. The sting remains. And another hurt happens. The marriage begins to grow seeds of misunderstanding and resentment.

In response we start to protect ourselves from the pain we feel. We avoid sharing our hearts in a transparent way. We cover up our feelings with a busy life. We try to control our spouse somehow to minimize the next potential hurt. We blame the other person for the way our relationship feels.

We begin to believe they are the problem. If only they would change, we could have the successful marriage we want. We sit on the opposite side of the table seeing our spouse as the enemy. We want them to meet our needs. We want them to love us.

If only we could avoid this. But no matter how hard we try we can't because no one is perfect. Added to this, our world brings a myriad of hardships that reveal our inabilities to love perfectly.

The only way forward is Team. It's a choice. We need to move our chair—literally and emotionally—from across the table to the place next to our spouse. It's not easy, and it's not perfect; many times it's not pretty, but it's the first step toward success.

How do we get there?

Many have said to me, "How can I do this? How can I be Team with this person who has hurt me so deeply for so long?"

The tricky part about marriage is that even though it

involves two people, we can only choose how one of them will relate: ourselves. We can't choose for the other person. Sometimes the other chooses to walk away. Or their actions cause a break that is irreparable. For those who are in that place, I offer you grace and love. May you know that you worked as much as possible; you did what could be done for the sake of your team.

I don't offer what follows as a panacea for every problem, but as principles to be applied with wisdom and discernment. Many times, this is done best with trusted friends, counselors and professional help. For those of us wanting to choose "Team," we have to start with ourselves.

The first crucial step to take is to forgive. Forgiveness means we let go of the desire to make our spouse pay. It doesn't mean what they did was right. It means that we stop requiring them to pay for their wrong. We also accept that we are in need of forgiveness as well. Both of us are imperfect. Both of us need love.

This process of forgiveness includes saying the words, "I forgive" or "I let go of making them pay," as well as deep heart work. It is a one-time decision (done a thousand times), and then also a lifetime of choosing to live it out. Forgiving one area often exposes another layer where it is needed. No matter who you are, it will be necessary, and it is easier said than done. Inviting God or another person into this forgiveness process helps.

Following forgiveness work, we are prepared to take the next step.

We want "Team," so we choose to act like a teammate.

We want honor, so we start speaking with dignity.

We want openness, so we share our heart with the other.

We want faithfulness, so we choose to think faithfully.

We want patience, so we wait and listen.

We want understanding, so we ask questions and rephrase what we hear.

Imagine if...

You shared your needs or fears with kindness?

You confessed your desire to get your own needs met first?

You surrendered your demands and listened?

You faced the problems together?

We are always stronger together. An ancient poet said it well, "By yourself you're unprotected. With a friend you can face the worst."

Mary and her husband kept a small practice that reinforced their choice to be Team for each other. They wrote daily notes of encouragement, "I love you," "I will guard you above all others" and "You are delightful to me."

Diana does a regular check in to see if her heart is open or closed to her husband. She imagines her heart as a door, and when it is closed to him, she prays for help to open the door. At times, she wanted to keep the door shut, but for forty-eight years she chose openness. Looking back, she would tell you she is glad she did.

My husband and I discovered that talking about our hurts brings us back to Team. We share our hearts honestly, listen and reflect back what we are hearing. This takes minutes, and sometimes days or weeks.

We're twenty-two years into marriage. It's better, and deeper, and harder, and more wonderful than ever. And we're doing it together, facing the brokenness—in ourselves and in the world together—as Team.

As you choose Team for your marriage, you get the privilege to offer lifegiving love to your spouse. You can also invite your partner to be Team with you. It won't be easy; it will require lots of practice and maybe even a coach, and yet it will be worth it! I believe that if you choose Team, you too can experience a beautiful and successful marriage.

ABOUT THE AUTHOR

Anna Stager is a Certified Coach & Author who helps heart-focused, authentic women and couples thrive.

Her own story is one of moving from hardship and struggle to abundance and wholeness. As a wife and mom Anna faced challenges in different circumstances: living overseas, infertility, adoption, special needs parenting, full time ministry and major health battles. While in these trials, she learned how to move from fear and overwhelm to a place of joy and peace.

Now, Anna's passion and joy is to provide help and hope in the midst of hardship. She provides coaching and specific resources to guide others from living in discouragement and overwhelm to living with joy, purpose and peace.

Connect with her at www.annastager.com

17

THE TRUTH ABOUT SUCCESS AS A SINGLE MOM

LA SHEONDA SANCHEZ

I know exactly where we were when it happened. We were driving to lunch after church to meet some friends. And from the back seat of the car, my three-year-old daughter declared, "Mama, I want to go be like Nemo and find my daddy."

She broke my heart that day.

I never wanted to be with her father again, but I knew the desire of her heart was to know her daddy.

When I told her father that I was pregnant, I was given an ultimatum. Abortion. Or do it alone. So, I chose to do it alone.

At the point when my daughter asked me that question, I had already been doing it alone for a few years. Being a single mom is one of the hardest things I have ever had to do. But it is also the absolute best thing I have ever done. The world is a better place with my daughter in it. I am a better person because God chose me to be her mother.

From the time I knew I was pregnant, I wanted to do the very best for the child I was carrying.

When Cassidy came into the world, she changed my name to Mama, and I have never been the same.

When they laid her in my arms, I wanted to do and be the very best for her even more. Like every parent, I was painfully aware of the many mistakes I made, bad choices navigated, and tough situations survived.

The absolute best choice that any single parent can make is to stay in community with others. And that can look differently for everyone.

Community is a pretty broad idea. For Cassidy and me, it was our church first and foremost. We had friends in the very church I had been attending since childhood. We made new friends there who were also part of single-parent families.

We had a small group Bible study. That group was our life-line. We would have Bible study during the week together, but it was so much more. We attended church together, but also shared meals, talked to each other outside of church, went places like fairs, movies, and coffeehouses.

We did life together.

Community is family. Both by blood and by choice. Most importantly for me, community means staying in connection with God. Without a relationship with God, our story would have turned out so differently. Raising my daughter in our faith, with the knowledge that God has a plan for her life and a plan for my life, is what gave us hope. The path in front of a single parent can often feel darkened with discouragement. The light of hope was welcome as our next steps often felt uncertain.

When you are in community, friends sense when your life is not going well. And they often offer to help. My self-sufficiency could have been our downfall. But I finally learned how to accept help. As a single parent, accepting help is not a sign of weakness. Instead, it is a sign of wisdom, honesty, and love for your child. You can still know how capable you are in the midst of asking someone else for help.

God's plan for a family is to include two parents. We were not meant to carry the awesome weight of parenthood alone. You are going to need help when there is no one else in the bullpen—so ask.

I remember praying, regularly, that I would be the very best mother in the world. Not out of pride, but because that is what I wanted for my daughter. And I remember, because I know my own faults all too well, asking God to make my mistakes and flaws slide off of Cassidy like Teflon.

I prayed that prayer regularly.

Recently, I asked Cassidy what she remembers about being raised by a single mom. Both the good and the bad. She is now in college but was quickly able to tell me that she honestly could not remember anything bad.

Since I know the mountains of missteps that I made along the way, I know that this is nothing more or less than answered prayer. God helped block out all the times I screwed up as a mom and as a human.

One thing Cassidy did tell me that she remembers while being raised by a single mom was that we spent lots of time together. Yet another example of community. And community with your child (or with your children) is unsurpassed in importance when you are a single parent.

We had rituals and traditions, most of which were incredibly silly, looking back. But that is what bound us together as family. And it is what we look back on now, remember together, and laugh about.

We would go on mommy-daughter dates. Sometimes that would be at a restaurant or movie, but many times we did not spend a dime. We took our dog for walks in the neighborhood, played at the playground in the park, and looked at the stars from our backyard.

I learned that sometimes a clean house could just wait. I wanted swept floors and folded laundry and a perfect lawn.

And we definitely worked on her learning chores and responsibilities. But we also learned to take some time and spend it together in lieu of chores and cleaning.

Forgiveness is another key. Forgiving Cassidy's father was a process.

Rushing that forgiveness will not yield results but has to be done. I also had to look in the mirror and forgive the woman there.

And forgiving myself...that was even harder. The key became learning and then allowing myself to move on rather than getting stuck in the past.

It is easy to allow loneliness to tempt you into ill-advised situations and relationships. That is why it is so important to keep living! We went to every strawberry festival, Irish dance troupe performance, local fair, and farmers market we could find. We went with just the two of us and other times we went with friends.

I dreamed of someday being married and having a larger family. Just as Cassidy dreamed of knowing her daddy. But we did not sit at home feeling sorry for ourselves.

We had community.

And I had forgiven.

But one more key to our thriving? Gratitude.

Be grateful for the gift of your child. Be grateful for the shelter you have, whatever that looks like. Be grateful for your most recent meal. Be grateful for the second-hand clothes, beat-up car, and frozen dinners. Express that gratitude. And really feel it.

Being grateful will lift your spirits on days when you feel helpless and hopeless.

I also had to take the time to heal.

Heal from the hurt of abandonment in pregnancy. Heal from the wounds in my past. Wounds that had allowed me to put myself in the position to become a single mother to begin with.

I first had to realize and acknowledge that I needed healing. And then I had to do the work. Emotional, spiritual, relational work.

Following that, I started taking care of myself physically. How I ate. Prioritizing exercise. Staying active.

Choosing to allow people closer than an arm's length distance.

I did not date anyone for many years. When I finally healed enough to start letting people in, I only went on two dates. Two first dates. And these happened when Cassidy was a few years into elementary school.

I had dating rules, though. Neither of those dates was allowed to meet Cassidy. Because someone would have to make it a whole lot longer than a single date for me to introduce them to my daughter.

But then Michael, an old friend from high school, asked me to lunch.

We had never dated—had only been friends. But we remained friends after high school. Since this was not a "date," and it was just lunch with an old friend, I brought Cassidy. And he was absolutely comfortable with Cassidy coming. The three of us had a great lunch. I remember Cassidy calling Michael my "ninja friend" after a little ramekin of sauce had fallen off the table, and he caught it in midair without spilling a drop.

This casual, but life-changing lunch led to Michael being my date to a wedding in which Cassidy was a flower girl. And this led to him becoming my boyfriend. He had been a loyal friend in high school. And now he was teaching Cassidy to ride a bike and play catch.

I recall one particular spring afternoon after we had been dating just a few months. Cassidy asked Michael when she could call him Daddy.

My heart stopped.

And without skipping a beat, he told her he loved her.

Nothing could have made me feel more loved than watching him love my daughter.

He told her she could call him Daddy that day or next week or next month or anytime she wanted to.

So naturally we heard Cassidy call him Daddy about thirty-seven times in the next hour.

Michael is now my husband and we have more children together.

And the search for Nemo's daddy was successful. It may have been a little different from the movie, but it culminated in a happy ending just the same.

ABOUT THE AUTHOR

As a former single mom and wife who has blended families, La Sheonda guides women in maximizing family life without losing themselves in the process. From cooking workshops to meal preps and instructional videos to meal plans with recipes and grocery lists, La Sheonda makes delicious dishes easy to incorporate into the family dinner table. As the founder of Saving Grace Suppers and Crunchy on a Curve, she empowers women with tools to feed their families while saving their time and sanity. La Sheonda is a Bible study leader who shares truths from God's Word that are the sustenance every soul craves. Her degree in Bible pales in comparison to her relationship with its Author. She lives in Texas with her three daughters, husband, two dogs, and as many chickens as she can get away with. Connect with her at www.lasheonda.com

18

THE TRUTH ABOUT SUCCESSFULLY GIVING YOURSELF GRACE THROUGH MOTHERHOOD

KOREEN CHANDLER

Why do I do this? The words swirled around my head as tears stung the back of my eyes and threatened to spill over. All I could see was fear staring back at me through four sets of eyes attached to the precious little treasures God had blessed me and my husband with. *Oh Aaron, if there was ever a time I needed you to be home, it is now,* I whispered to myself as the tears built up enough fury to slowly trickle down my cheeks.

I started racking my brain to figure out what had brought me here, to this moment, when I was ashamed of myself, ashamed of the mommy I thought I had become.

The day had started out like every morning had the last few months. I woke up with a knot in my neck from our bed being invaded with our four little ones and our white lab. I smiled to myself and thought the only thing that could have made that moment sweeter would have been if Aaron's work boots were neatly in their place, but they weren't. They were across the world.

A wave of emotions flooded over me. Being married to a soldier comes with its own mixture of sweet and bitter emotions.

Moments of feeling overly blessed to be married to a man who loves not only his God and family with every ounce of his being but his country too. Pride in being married to a man who chooses to serve all three of his loves with his whole heart every minute of every day. The pride in my littles' eyes as I explain to our boys (three and four years old, respectively), who love a good "hero and villain story" that *their daddy* is a real-life superhero.

But there is another emotional side to being married to a soldier. A deep feeling of being alone. The constant ball of nerves in my stomach when he is deployed. Waking up alone to raise our four little treasures...alone. With the continuous prayer that never really stops in my heart: "Dear Father, PLEASE keep him safe."

The loneliness and pain from my soulmate not being here can be very overwhelming. Him not being around to see our precious toddler girls smash through milestones faster than I can blink. He can never get those moments back. Our girls can never get that time back, and he misses it.

Add in the whole "get to know daddy" through the very limited time frame of FaceTime calls, and then I realized it. I pinpointed where I'd started out my day with my own little ball of worried nerves already wound up tight.

My littles started to stir, and a solo of the song that got stuck on repeat called, "I'm starving, Mommy" turned into a trio with my littlest grunting and pointing towards the door. Her way of informing me she wanted to turn that trio into a quartet.

Adding a layer of guilt to my already tight nerve ball, I thought to myself, *I really need to be better at making sure I get my backside out of bed fast enough to have breakfast ready for them.*

I quickly snapped into mommy-mode and got morning potty time done and diapers changed.

I got everyone sitting down and prayed that things would go

smoothly. *Of all days, Father, please just let today go smoothly for my already wound-up nerves.*

I decided that since all the littles were distracted with their chocolate milk and oatmeal, I would quickly clean the floors, which was a chore I had had on my list two days earlier but could never seem to squeeze in.

When I think back, I added a layer of feeling inadequate to my ball of messy nerves. I felt like I was a bad mommy who could not figure out how to keep a house clean.

It was a balancing act for sure, refereeing our eldests, as we call them: our four-year-old boy and our two-year-old girl, who both carry a heavy dose of the eldest-child syndrome. And there was me, just hurrying to make sure I could get the floors done before I had to stop and wash oatmeal mustaches and beards off faces.

Right here I add a layer of stress to my already wound-up ball of nerves.

Luckily, as I finished mopping the last few tiles in the hall I heard my eldest yelling for me, "Mommy my belly is happy." I grabbed a wash rag and started cleaning his face, which then turned into a mass cleaning of all four of their faces, their hands, the table, the chairs, the floor, the ceiling, the top of the dog's head.... Okay, it was not that bad but it sure felt like they got oatmeal everywhere except their mouths.

After the last of them was cleaned up, I turned to my next project—the never-ending, bottomless pit of dishes.

I put on my nice mommy voice and asked my little tornadoes, who were creating a huge mess in the once-clean living room, to go to their play room, a designated space we set up specifically for them to "destroy" to their hearts' content.

They listened just long enough for me to get half of the top rack of the dishwasher cleared out, and then I had to stop again to go play referee.

Why can they not just get along for five minutes so I can get these stupid dishes done?

I came back to the kitchen to find my itty-bitty with her cheeks pooching out like a chipmunk.

I walked over to her, slipping on the dog water she'd decided to play in as she smiled up at me innocently as if to say, "You do not see anything, Mommy." I growled to myself and muttered under my breath, "*Seriously,*" and added another layer of guilt. *I really need to watch her more carefully so she does not choke on something.*

I calmly told her to spit it out and out popped eight pieces of slobbery, partially chewed-up dog food. She had apparently decided that she was still hungry and, hey, if the dog liked it, she would too, right?

I walked back to the dishwasher to keep chipping away at my task. As I successfully emptied the dishwasher, I heard my eldest three messing and playing in the living room again.

Add another layer of anger to my ball of nerves. *Why do they never listen to me?*

My patience with them was wearing thin, but I mustered up enough of it to make sure I again had my nice-mommy voice on while I asked them, a second time, to go to their playroom.

They ignored me.

I asked them again a little bit more sternly while I turned back to the sink full of dishes. I rinsed out a sippy cup with the previous day's milk residue still in it and placed it in the dishwasher while the anger grew.

Then, it happened.

I heard a crash and saw three little culprits sneak away from my once-clean living room. In its place I found an overturned table and three sippies previously filled with chocolate milk missing their lids. The contents were strewn all over my freshly mopped living room and painting my white walls.

I lost it.

I started yelling...at the top of my lungs. I continued yelling at them about how they'd ruined my freshly cleaned floor and how long it took me to clean it and why can they never listen, and why can they not just be good and make good choices for five minutes so I can get these stupid dishes done?

Then, in the midst of my yelling, I realized that I was not just yelling; I was screaming, and a wave of guilt swept over me as my children's eyes stared at me in fear. They slowly backed away from me and ran down the hall to their playroom, crying because Mommy was "scary and mean."

I held back the tears and whispered to myself, *I'm such a bad mommy, why do I have to yell at them like that? When did I turn into such a bad mommy? I am nowhere near being the Proverbs-31 mommy I pray daily to be. Aaron, please come home.*

Does my story sound familiar? Maybe switch a few details around because, hey, we are all unique, but I know I am not the only mommy who has had what I call "bad-mommy moments."

I'm here to tell you, Mama, that a bad-mommy moment does not make you a bad mommy.

The trick is to humble yourself, go to the playroom, scoop your babies up, and apologize for losing your temper.

Explain how you were in the wrong and the way you reacted was wrong.

USE your "bad-mommy moment" as a teaching opportunity.

Since that day, my "bad-mommy moment" is where I have really been focusing on my personal growth. I do not ever want those moments to control me again. When I feel what I like to call my "mean-mommy voice" coming, I take a deep breath and try to find something I am grateful for before opening my mouth.

The more you practice this, the more control you will have over your "mean-mommy voice."

I do not know about you, but one of my ultimate goals in life is to be the Proverbs-31 mommy. Verse 38 says, "Her children arise up, and call her blessed; her husband also, and he praiseth her."

I want my little treasures to remember me keeping my head in a stressful situation. I want them rising up every morning thankful that I AM their mommy. I want them to see what a good mommy looks like so they in turn can be good parents.

I realized when this day happened that I never wanted a repeat of it, so I started down a path of personal development. Working on the mommy I knew God saw me to be. Working on the mommy I know I am.

Did you know your emotions are like an onion, and if you do not deal with things that give you an emotional charge your subconscious creates what are called "inner rules" to protect you from feeling angry (or sad, scared, ashamed—you insert a feeling) anymore?

During my reflecting on that day, I realized that was where my problem lie. I would feel a negative feeling, then hear a negative voice in response to that feeling and dwell on it. Creating a huge ball of messy nerves that eventually exploded on the people I hold dearest to my heart.

I stumbled on to a personal development tool by Dr. Benjamin Perkus called the Aroma Freedom Technique, in which you use essential oils to go in and release the negative emotions and inner rules you have holding you back from being the person God created you to be. I would be lying if I told you that I have arrived and I no longer have what I call "bad-mommy moments," but I can tell you that every day God blesses me to hear my littles' voices is another day I am using the Aroma Freedom Technique to clear out the negative "layers" I have built up over the years. I CONTROL those moments instead of them controlling me.

This personal development tool helped me so much I

decided to become an aroma freedom practitioner myself, so that I can be a blessing to all those mommies out there who felt like me—a bad mommy.

I am now blessed to have the tool to not only work on me, but help mommies out there realize that a bad-mommy moment does not make you a bad mommy!

Each day and every day, with God's help and this new technique, I am taking one step closer to being the Proverbs-31 mommy I know God sees me to be.

ABOUT THE AUTHOR

Koreen is a God loving, happily married, blessed mother to 4 littles. She is an Aroma Freedom Practitioner, Published Author, Aspiring Podcaster, and an influential optimistic Entrepreneur. Koreen's passion is helping mothers find their way back to being who God sees them to be by helping them clear out negative thoughts feelings and emotions. She also loves helping women achieve their goals that seem just out of reach by guiding them through Aroma Freedom sessions helping them breakthrough roadblocks they have created for themselves. Aroma Freedom is an empowering and life changing technique Koreen uses not only on others but also on herself to help her achieve her own personal development journey towards being a Proverbs 31 wife and mother. You can connect with Koreen or schedule an Aroma Freedom session with her at KoreenChandler.com

19

THE TRUTH ABOUT SUCCESSFULLY INTEGRATING YOUR KIDS INTO BUSINESS

JILL COLETTI

The moment I told my boss, a sense of calm took over my body and I let out the biggest exhalation ever. I was escaping groundhog-day and would soon be free to create the life I had been dreaming about for myself and my kids.

I knew it was the "right" move for me when I felt it in my gut. I mean, anytime I had given notice at a job in the past, the tears would flow. But not this time. No more missing out on important moments with my kids. No more revolving my life around someone else's schedule and influence. I was taking my power back. I was honoring myself and my priorities with the intention to be more present for my kids and to inspire and empower them in the process.

Now, this did not happen overnight. I had been dreaming about giving my notice just a little over a year after working for the company and I was there for eleven and a half years. Great company, great people but I knew deep down in my soul that my life was meant to go in a different direction. I just had no idea what it was or how to find it. I took the job because I felt I should. I was married and my husband and I had plans that required more income. It was a decently paying job at a large company with lots of benefits and potential to move up. I was doing what I was good at. But I did not enjoy what I was doing.

When I got pregnant about a year and a half into the job, I kept wondering how I could go back to work after having a child. Then I had her, and that first day back to work after maternity leave was absolutely awful. I held back tears while working, and every break I had was spent pumping and sobbing for weeks. I was leaving my daughter with people she did not know and missing out on a huge chunk of her young life while I worked at a job where if something happened to me today, they would fill my cubicle with someone else tomorrow. I was replaceable at work BUT I was not replaceable at home. This feeling lingered and lingered, but I felt that I could not do anything about it. I had to work.

Years went by. I would wake up, mindlessly get myself dressed, get the kids ready, drive to daycare then to work. I would work all day only to rush out to drive to daycare, feed the kids, put them to bed, fall asleep on the couch from exhaustion then repeat. Day in and day out, that was my life. I felt lost and overwhelmed. I did not know who I was anymore. I had dreams, but they were only dreams. I didn't think they would ever come true.

I had no confidence, no direction and no drive to pursue them. Life was just happening to me, and the worst part was that I had so many hopes for my kiddos, but I was not the mom I dreamt of being for them. *How could I help them pursue an amazing life if I was not living one?*

Add divorce into the picture and this was not the life I had planned or signed up for.

Or was it?

I truly believe that everything and everyone I have experienced in the entire forty-four years of my life happened *for* me and were meant to teach me and support me as my soul evolves.

I have absolutely no regrets and know that I am the person that I am because of all I have witnessed and experienced. Though getting to this mindset did not happen overnight.

After my divorce, I began searching. Searching for dreams, inspiration, desires; for the true authentic ME. I did not know who I was anymore, or what I even liked to do or feel. Now I had more time to figure myself out. The searching led me to an amazing fitness and life coach who I thought was going to whip my body into shape because losing weight was going to "fix" me. Ha-ha! I had no idea what I was getting myself into.

Did I learn a ton about nutrition and lose some weight? Yes, but that did not help me as much as exploring my spirituality did. The key for me was rediscovering my connection to the universe, forming daily non-negotiable spiritual practices, trusting my intuition again, and most of all setting the "mom guilt" aside and putting myself first.

When I put myself first it not only helped me but helped my kids and everyone else around me. What? YES! Read that last sentence again. Taking care of me first did not take anything away from my kids, but rather it gave them more than I could have imagined.

I will never forget the day my kids told me, with a light in their eyes, how happy they were to see me so happy. My heart melted. They were noticing a change in me. I was rediscovering who I was. I was becoming the mom that I desired to be. And I was showing them, through example, how to value themselves too. We are worthy as we are. God made us for a reason. Wow, the pride I felt in that moment. It had been a while since I felt so proud of myself.

My spiritual awakening was the start of finding my purpose and beginning my journey towards creating an amazing high-vibe legacy *for* my kids and *with* my kids. My kids will not only witness what I am doing, but they will participate too.

So that day in my boss's office, I announced to her that I was leaving the corporate world for a life of spiritual entrepreneur-ship. And, by the way, my kids helped guide this decision. I was done repeating the same day over and over. My life was happening to me not for me. I was missing out. I desired to be inspired *every* day. I desired to be intentional with my time and my energy. I desired to help empower others. Starting my own business was the answer I had been looking for. Bridging my higher consciousness with my kids, my life and my now my work. I can be with my kids every day on my terms, not someone else's. It was not easy, but it was simple. I can be me and do me every day. When I jumped on the entrepreneurship rollercoaster, my kids jumped on with me. There are no age or height requirements on my ride. Though fear may rear its head, we will have fun riding all the ups and downs, and we will learn along the way.

As I am writing this, my seven-year-old son just snuck out of bed and asked, "Mom, what are you doing?" This is not new to us; he has all the questions at night, and according to him is never tired when it's bedtime. If you are a mom, you know what I mean. When I responded that I was writing this chapter he said, "but I wanted to do that with you, Mom."

My heart skipped a beat and part of me almost caved and let him stay up. Instead, I told him how much I would love to and promised him that we would write together the next night. And we did. His book is all about taking action; inspired by the movies, he says. "You know, Mom, when the actors keep going until they get the scene right? Like when we never give up in our life, Mom." Insert proud-mom moment with maybe a few tears. You are right, buddy. If we desire something in our life, we take action and we do not give up until we make it happen. This is something that our journey to following our purpose together has taught us.

My business has led not only to freedom of time, location, and soon finances, but has also connected me to my kids in so many ways. I have been able to spend quality time with them. I have been able to teach them about business planning, finance, marketing, creation, time management, book writing, leading with service to others and more.

The kids help me brainstorm ideas for merchandise and content, they help me file and do the more mundane stuff, they jump on videos from time to time when we are sharing pieces of our life, and they even help keep me accountable by reminding me to stay on task. We meditate together, set intentions, create visions and mastermind together. The kids are my number one tribe. They are the glue in my foundation. Yes, I have taught them, but truly I believe they have taught me so much more.

I have been able to show them that they can do anything they set their minds to. If their forty-four-year-old mama can flip her life around and start afresh by pursuing her dreams, so can they at any age. (And so can you by the way...) They can start a business, write a book, lead a discussion, teach a class and so much more. The sky is the limit.

We have learned things through this business that school may never be able to teach us: self-worth, confidence, perseverance, motivation; all while connecting with each other and helping others. Oh, and by the way, my daughter not only started her own business at eleven years old during a pandemic, but she also helps me with mine and is in the process of writing a book too!

The kids see my wins as well as the lessons I learn. They have seen growth and setbacks. They are my biggest encouragers when I could use a boost, and they celebrate every single little win big with me. Times have been tough in some ways, and through it all we live in gratitude as we continue to design and pursue an extraordinary life and legacy. And that is the definition of success to me.

ABOUT THE AUTHOR

Jill is a Multidimensional Healer, Coach, Content Creator & Spiritual Mama. She empowers moms to design a life they love and create an extraordinary legacy **for** their kids **with** their kids.

Jill's personal healing journey inspired her to make changes in her life that have helped her and her family find more love, joy & abundance. The impact of this was so great that she left her corporate career to start her own business focused on helping families heal too.

When we heal and take care of ourselves, we heal the world around us. Let's shift the energy of this world together! Are you ready?

Connect with her at www.jillcoletti.com

20

THE TRUTH ABOUT SUCCESSFULLY RAISING FIVE GIRLS WITH ONE BATHROOM

RACHEL TIBOLD

M um of five, Domestic Engineer, MBA (masters in babies & adolescents), that's me. I had business cards made with that title on them because 1. It was a great conversation starter, and 2. It was so much easier than digging for a pen and paper in my purse, backpack or diaper bag. I thought it was brilliant. Work smarter, not harder.

Raising five daughters is an adventure all on its own. An adventure I am proud to say I have survived and performed well. There is no manual, and they're not born with instructions. You have to basically wing it for the next eighteen-or-so years. Parents have their way of raising their kids. Each generation knows better than the one before, or so they think. Many have even written books and guides. Somehow, the little humans turn out okay. Just remember, it's an adventure.

Now, raising five daughters and being a blended family is definitely an adventure. The girls were six and seven years old when we married. He was a widower, and I was a single mom. Just as fate & faith had brought us all together, fate & faith decided we needed three more girls in our family. Suddenly, I was stepmom, then adopted mom, preemie mom and mom. To us and to all the kids, being "blended" really didn't change anything. We didn't see our family as separate units. There was never talk of "step" or "half." We were just family. They were sisters, and all my kids knew it and lived it. We had no idea what we were in for. We just knew we had faith, family, friends, community, but more importantly, we had each other. These are just some things that make up the foundation that I've used on numerous occasions to get by. They all kind of merge into one another and back out to be their own thing. Whatever faith/religious belief/ higher power you have, use it as a foundation to learn and grow. The family, friends and community with which you surround yourself shape you. They are the emotional, physical, and spiritual support that is needed and all intertwined.

Do your best and give your all in all you do. Be a good friend and neighbor and definitely be a good citizen. We all know what to do. Take care of others, especially those in need. Go out into your community and volunteer at missions and shelters, soup kitchens, and food banks. Join community outreach programs.

Five daughters, all in a modest home (split-level raised ranch) with ONE bathroom. Yes, ONE bathroom. (Remember, we are on an adventure. No one said it was going to be easy.) You soon learn to wake up real early or shower in the evening, brush your teeth in the kitchen sink or while someone else is showering. We had three girls in one bedroom with their beds lined up in a U shape. They had bunk beds, loft beds, canopy, princess beds. We had great imaginations. Someone wanted a privacy pod and it ended up looking like a Tardis. We had bed tents too. Our house was never empty. Extended family and friends knew our space was their space. We had an open door and extra plates at the table. No one went hungry or got left out.

Throughout the years of raising five daughters, I really had to be prepared for the unexpected and use my intuition and instinct. Many times we just went off-the-cuff and that is totally okay. Remember there are no manuals. It's an adventure.

You learn early on that sharing is caring (thank you, care-bears). We did our best to respect space and time. Sometimes those things just clashed. We have holes in our linen closet door to remind us. No one has really admitted to kicking it in, but it's just a small reminder. A reminder to think of the next person waiting...

Babies, toddlers, (in-betweens), teens...oh my! Babies are blessings. Let's just keep it short. They eat, pee, poop, sleep and repeat.

Moving on to toddlers. These are the years when, some say, their brains are like sponges. They see, hear, and repeat every-thing. This is also the stage where testing your patience is going to happen. It's okay. You have a community of awesome people and resources, use them. What a great age for exploring, espe-cially when they want to be a wild animal at bedtime. Just roll with it.

Oh, is that a new fad? Ha, no; those are just hair ties on my wrist. Hair ties everywhere. If you need one, I've got plenty. Doing hair was pretty easy for me. I had a mannequin head growing up, so I can whip up French braids and updos. At one time, we had every hair crimper, curler and straightener under that one sink.

Oh, the teen years. I remember the adventure well! You survived the toddler and tween years. You can do this. Where is my sweet child, and what have you done with her? I had a motto, "Hate me now, love me later." It's okay, their brains are still developing. They eventually come back to you and realize you were right all along, and they do need your love and guid-ance. I guess it's not about who is right and wrong. It's more, "I respect your opinion and I'm going to give you the space to figure it out." Yes, eventually it all works out.

Hiking trips and outdoor activities seem to be the go-to for kids and teens. Keep it simple. Geocaching and treasure hunting, trees, creeks, mud, breathing in the fresh air. All the elements for a great day for any age. We'd go on holiday mornings. Even now, as young adults, it's one of the things they all get together and still do.

At some point I realized this is my life. Stop, go, repeat. I am MOM. The sleepless nights, the laughs and cries. All of it is so worth it.

Within this adventure, you've given them a strong foundation to be present in this world today. Raise them to become kind, compassionate humans who are merciful and kind to *all*.

You have to remember to trust your instincts and follow your intuitions. You all have it inside. It is a matter of finding it and believing it. Amazing things can happen when we believe in ourselves. When you are running on empty and finding that you are doubting yourself and your abilities, be kind to yourself. Read that again: Be kind to yourself. Take some time for you. Go for a walk, read a book, meditate, exercise, eat your favorite food, listen to your favorite music. It doesn't have to take a lot of your time to find the balance. Find balance in everything you do.

Pretty soon another day is on the horizon, filled with shared stories of faith, traditions, love, and pictures of the past in our minds. A little piece of us, our memories.

Just breathe! It's okay. The adventure is going to be great. Believe in yourself, because I believe in you.

ABOUT THE AUTHOR

Rachel is a wife, mother of 5 daughters, artist, doula & future podcaster. She is an independent consultant, collaborator, retreat/workshop facilitator, keynote speaker & community builder. She is a trained Spiritual Healer through C.A.R.E. using Young Living Essential Oils specializes in Raindrop Technique, Vitaflex, & Emotional Release. She specializes in Birth & Post-partum Care as well as multigenerational support.

As a self care/support/breath coach, her goal for your wellness journey is to foster an experience that offers you emotional, physical, and informational support, so that you feel empowered to make choices that meet your needs.

Connect with Rachel here: racheltibold.com

V

HEALTH & HOPE

21

THE TRUTH ABOUT SUCCESS IN YOUR HEALTH

JO PRONGER FAULKNER

When I first told my family doctor I was going to make myself better, I knew he didn't believe me. In that moment, he barely acknowledged what I said, let alone try to offer any advice, or even try talk me out of it, for that matter. He only mumbled, "Mmm hmm," while staring at his computer screen, trying to determine which of my daily prescriptions needed renewing. I pulled the pill bottles from my purse and pointed to the ones that were low.

Back in 2012, I was my doctor's first patient diagnosed with systemic lupus erythematosus, and two years later, his first patient with mixed connective tissue disease. Each of these conditions is difficult to diagnose and manage. On top of having them both, I also had a malfunctioning thyroid, and complex regional pain syndrome. I'm pretty certain he didn't think "better" was possible, and at that point, I don't think I did either. I desperately wanted to get my health back. I just wasn't sure I would ever figure out how.

My pain had been getting progressively worse. I lacked energy and often felt achy and run-down like I had the flu. I felt a sharp pain in my hips when walking, and even when I tried riding my horse. I had intermittent pain and swelling in other joints. I experienced frequent headaches, rashes, my voice would come and go (often accompanied by a sore throat), I had random stabbing eye pain, and brain fog. No matter how exhausted I felt, I had a hard time falling asleep before one or two o'clock in the morning. I often got sick with coughs, colds, and bronchitis. I also suffered with frequent urinary tract infections. On top of multiple daily prescriptions I was told I had to take for life, plus antibiotics every month or two for the various infections, I also took several over-the-counter pain relievers every day. All of these symptoms made my finance job—sitting at a computer, working on spreadsheets—next to impossible.

This was my life for years. Some weeks were better than others and I could get myself to work, while other weeks I would spend mostly in bed. I tried to make the best of things when I saw friends and family, and would put on my happiest smile for holidays, birthday dinners and social media selfies— but I was secretly contemplating how to end my life. After not being able to come up with "the best" way to do that without it being traumatizing for whoever found me, I figured I might as well try something else first.

My health had suffered for so long, by the time I blurted out the words in the doctor's office that day in 2016, I knew I needed a different approach. I was "done" with medications that caused the same side effects as the actual symptoms of the autoimmune conditions I had. Done fighting with my boss who constantly requested medical documentation, yet insisted I return to work. Done with chronic stress from my ex who, for two years after our breakup, didn't want to sort things out amicably.

When I finally came to the conclusion that no one else was going to make me better, that no one else had as much at stake in my outcome as I did, and that ultimately I was the one in charge of everything that happens in my life, my paradigm shifted. This isn't to say I was elated at first about this lightbulb moment. In fact, it was perhaps the lowest point in my life. I was in the midst of what I figured was a midlife crisis: a complex, stressful divorce, friendship losses, a job loss, and my health was circling the drain. I had been chronically exhausted for years despite prescriptions that were supposed to be "helping." I was angry and frustrated that my doctors didn't have suggestions on alternatives which might be safer and more effective than additional drugs.

I wanted a "shake-up;" a new beginning. With the guidance of my rheumatologist and pharmacist, I began to gradually reduce my prescription dosages with the intent of completely weaning from them. When my health remained stable despite the lower doses, my boyfriend Mike and I headed off for a big adventure: We went to Big Corn Island, Nicaragua, to start building a vacation home. After his divorce and mine, we were both ready for a major shift in our new life together, and this was a pretty exciting one to focus on.

This was also around the time invasive melanoma (skin cancer) was added to the list of things I might die from. There was a delay in receiving my biopsy results and by the time I got the news months later, treatment was urgent. The surgeon removed a significant section of skin from my back, leaving an enormous, unsightly scar. The diagnosis and the medical procedure were devastating and scary, but I was brought to my senses by my friend Sonya Witherspoon, who was by my side through the entire experience. She gracefully reminded me that my scar was better than the alternative (dying from melanoma); that it would fade over time and I would get to go on living an adventurous life. I am forever grateful for her generous heart and her meaningful words at exactly the right time.

Our experience on Big Corn Island, which was the good part of a year, was the catalyst I so desperately needed to turn my health around. We were up with the rising sun and outside in the fresh Caribbean air all day long, and went to bed soon after sunset. I slept like a log every night and stopped needing daytime naps. The longer we were there, the better I felt and the more I was able to do throughout the day. We ate large quantities of fresh fruits and vegetables in every meal, rice and beans, hand-picked plantains, bananas and mangoes from our own trees, occasionally had some fresh fish or lobster, and we cooked with coconut oil. We drank natural electrolytes (coconut water), and tamarind juice (supporting for liver health). When we ate sandwiches, they were made with fresh, local coconut-flour bread, without wheat or preservatives. My digestive system had no issues at all with this new way of eating, compared to the daily bloating and gut pain I used to experience back home in Canada.

Before we drove to Nicaragua, and while we were there all those months working hard to "build our dream," some people told us we would never make it; we were crazy to try. Even when we returned to Canada, regretfully leaving the project unfinished for a period of time, people told us to just give up and not waste any more effort or money on this risky, ridiculous goal. Others cheered us on and said they would love to come visit us when the time was right.

The ones who rooted for our success, and who still root for our success, became our closest, favorite people. It sure makes a positive impact to your mindset when someone believes in you, doesn't it?

By the time we returned home, Mike and I both felt rejuvenated. No longer on any prescriptions, I hadn't experienced any autoimmune flares while we were in Nicaragua. I had not caught anyone's cold (even when our building crew all got sick), and had not experienced any bladder issues or infections either. I hadn't felt that good in years.

Fast forward to the summer of 2020. Out of sheer curiosity I decided to get my bloodwork checked to assess my autoimmune health. I hadn't needed a rheumatologist since 2016 due to maintaining an intentionally healthy lifestyle. Any symptoms I experience these days are mild, temporary, and manageable without medication.

As it turns out, my health looks pretty good on paper too. The nurse practitioner who reviewed my results and compared them to years prior asked me what I was doing to maintain my autoimmune health without prescriptions. My thyroid levels are normal, lupus isn't showing up on my bloodwork anymore, and although I still have elevated antibodies for mixed connective tissue disease, I don't feel sick. I don't have daily, debilitating symptoms anymore. I don't even get headaches or heartburn, and I don't need naps. I have been able to work full time as well as build several businesses. Mike and I were also able to get our vacation home finished and have new plans to build others.

My entire life has changed because I took responsibility for my own outcome and found my motivation to continue the lifestyle once I realized what helped turn my health around. The reason I share my story with you, and what inspires me to help other autoimmune warriors, is to be a beacon of hope and possibility.

When it comes to making health changes, or changes in any area of your life for that matter, decide what your vision is. How do you want things to change? What would you love your life to be like in six months, or a year from now? Everyone's "ideal life" looks different.

Is something holding you back when you think about change, or when you try to take action? A belief that you're just unlucky, or what you want isn't possible? Or that you don't know how to achieve it? Do you think you'll be judged if you are successful and lead a fulfilling, high-vibing life?

These negative thoughts are limiting beliefs—ways of thinking that prevent us from taking action. They cause us to give up on our goals and dreams. Whether you are afraid of failure (believing you won't feel better despite your efforts) or are afraid of success (it might feel too overwhelming if you feel great and have more energy), it's the same problem. You are carrying around false beliefs that are blocking you from the life you deserve to be living. Limiting beliefs can be suffocating and can prevent you from taking action that could lead to something big. We often don't give ourselves enough credit for our own capabilities, and we come up with all kinds of reasons why we aren't ready.

Allow yourself to have an open, curious mind about what's possible, align that openness with a commitment to take action, and do *something* each day to move you in the direction of your goal. If you want better health, taking action could include making a healthy, homemade meal, going for a walk, researching and reading about wellness from credible sources, purging pent-up emotions through journaling, using positive affirmations and calming essential oils for a mindset reset, or putting out a bowl of fruit each morning for snacking on during the day. The more actions you take on a consistent basis, the easier and more habitual they become, and the sooner you'll notice improvements.

The truth is no one else can succeed for you. Success is an *accomplishment* or *outcome* resulting from determined action. Someone else's accomplishment is their success. Your accomplishment, your outcome as a result of your intentional actions, is your success. We might each have help along the way in our journey, and if you've been blessed with that kind of support, it is something to be grateful for. But let's be honest. We can't put our feet up, sit back, avoid the hard stuff, and expect success. If you have been contemplating change and haven't yet started, take a moment now to ask, "What matters to me most in my life and why?" Self-reflection is how you will inevitably discover your strongest motivations, which will empower you to intentionally build the life you truly desire.

ABOUT THE AUTHOR

Jo Pronger Faulkner is an entrepreneur, animal-lover, and nature enthusiast living in northwestern Ontario, Canada with her fiancé Mike. They are foodies and adventure-seekers; obsessed with their pets, Caribbean travel, renovation projects, and vision boards.

Jo is the author of *The Autoimmune Warrior's Healing Key*, a motivational #1 Best Selling book about her struggle with autoimmune illness, how the endocrine system works, and her discovery of the healing power of plants. Jo's goal in sharing her story is to help thousands of autoimmune warriors get their health back and get their life back. Her mission is to inspire women to listen to their intuition, reclaim their personal power, and make intentional choices to live the life they truly desire. Connect with her at https://JoProngerFaulkner.com

22

THE TRUTH ABOUT SUCCESS IN WEIGHT LOSS

MEGAN DALE

I was five years old, when I said these words: "I want to wear that swimsuit." It was a bikini. The words that were spoken to me after that were like an arrow of darkness piercing my heart. The arrow created a hole that would only get bigger as I grew up. "People your size do not wear bikinis. You need to cover up your belly." Longing to fit in and be accepted, my little girl's heart quickly grabbed hold of the thought that in order to be accepted and loved I needed to be thin. Having a thin body meant you were a better person. This was the very beginning of my weight loss journey.

I was in the sixth grade and I remember getting on a scale in gym class. Can we all just stop right there for a moment? The gym teacher was not fit, and why on Earth are we weighing young girls in a classroom setting? But I digress...

After that class, a group of the cool kids were all standing around saying their weight. Many were less than ten pounds away from my weight, but they were under the dreaded "three-digit number." The horrible things that so easily spewed out of their mouths that day were crushing.

I took it to mean that they were better than I was because they had a lower number on the scale. Do you know what I did in that moment? I lied about my number. I didn't dare let them know because they were being so harsh. What I didn't understand back then was that their harsh judgement of my weighing a hundred pounds as a sixth-grader only came from them being taught that having a thin body somehow equaled being accepted and more loved.

That's when I found myself on my first diet. I called it the "green bean diet." It was from a doctor's office where I went to get help for the low thyroid levels that puberty threw me into. Basically, the only two things I remember liking on that plan were green beans and chicken. We all know that didn't last long. The journey of overcoming the poor body image and the devastation of wanting to lose weight continued. The hidden desire to be accepted only grew stronger.

According to the CDC, the prevalence of obesity was 42.4% in 2017~2018. In 2015, weight-loss companies earned $935.4 million in profit, and the industry was expected to hit $8 billion by 2020, IBISWorld reports. The solution isn't as easy as "drink this shake, eat this protein bar, or do this work out." Those don't fix the hurts of the five-year-old little girl inside all of us who longs to be fully seen and deeply loved. The truth about weight loss is that it's not about the food.

Did you know that you are inundated with more than 90,000 messages a day? The majority of them are telling us how we should do more so we can be better. Your peace will come when (insert a goal you want to reach). I'm here to stand up for the truth and say really loudly so that the girls in the back can hear me too:

"If you don't have peace in your body right now, it's not going to come when you fit into those skinny jeans three sizes smaller."

Let me say that again, "If you don't have peace in your body right now, it's not going to come when you fit into those skinny jeans three sizes smaller."

Where does your peace come from? Peter from the Bible was walking on water, looking at Jesus, and turned to looked at his surroundings. He took his eye off Jesus and he sank! It's no wonder why as a culture we are sinking. Where are our eyes? They are on the 90,000 messages being thrown our way, trying to tell us how to measure up to an unreachable measuring stick.

Here is what I know: Whether I weighed two hundred and fifty pounds or a hundred and fifty pounds, my peace did not change. Yes, I was in smaller-sized jeans. Yes, I was more confident, BUT my response to the circumstances around me was the same! My heart still raced, my shoulders still got tense, and the pit in my stomach was just as painful. Go right ahead and ask a woman you consider to be "skinny" what she hates about her body. She will start to rattle off her list of dislikes faster than you can blink your eyes. I know if you reached your ideal body size you think you would never have anything negative to say about it, but that's not the truth.

Eventually, I was looking down at two hundred and thirty pounds again. It wasn't about the food. It was about my ability to try softer, not harder. Every time I tried harder and missed a step, I was back to missing the step for days, weeks, or months. Have you ever been there?

Then I would get so disgusted with myself that I would dive in all over again to a "new plan." Because this time it was really going to happen. I was finally going to lose the weight. I was finally going to feel good in my skin.

Little did I know, I didn't need another try-harder program. Those only had me trying again, and again, and again. Each time confirming the negative self-talk I was hearing. "This will never happen for you! Who do you think you are trying to achieve that goal? You just weren't meant to be free. It's too hard. It's taking too long." Digging really deep would lead me to the thought, "What if you get there and you are still judged? You won't have your size as a shield from their judgement."

Going through yet another drive up wasn't about being hungry. What if underneath it all there was a girl reaching for food because she'd experienced rejection, and food was always there for her? What if it were a hidden response from only receiving connection for periods of time? The act of her binging on the "off plan" had nothing to do with food. Just like when you go to start a "new diet," and you have a last-chance meal before you start again. Savoring the flavor of that chocolate cake with chocolate icing and eating three pieces because you know when the alarm clock rings on Monday morning, it's game on to getting serious. It's not about the food, my friend.

As a man thinks, so is he. We will not achieve peace in our bodies until we believe we are worthy of the cross. He paid it all so we could walk in freedom, yet we consume food to avoid what's really going on in our hearts. We numb out, we run away, we emotionally eat, when what we really need is an encounter with the radical love of God.

The shield of extra adipose tissue around my hips wasn't protecting me from the judgement of others. The extra muffin top for me was actually an excuse to cling to a self-imposed strategy to keep my heart from hurting. It's not as if the knowledge of how to lose weight is lacking. Put less calories in, have more calories out and you will lose weight. Don't eat sugar, but instead eat more fruits and vegetables. Drink more water and less soda. Move your body rather than sit on the couch watching Netflix.

We are so connected with social media, yet our hearts long to be connected without judgement in all that we are. Every time I tried and slipped up, it often reminded me of something from my past that was linked to who I thought I was rather than something I had done. Those statements act as confirmation every time we step up to the plate to "try again." I'm here to tell you the truth so you can walk the path to lasting freedom. Your identity can only be found in the One who knitted you together in your mother's womb. The One who died on the cross for all your hurts, hang ups, and missteps. To achieve lasting peace in your body, you must know the truth about weight loss: It's not about food, it's about the heart.

One way to see success on this journey is from a non-scale victory. It's a celebration of a heart change. On a date with my husband, we were asking each other questions from a book we had.

I asked him, "What is a bad habit I have that you think I could work on?"

His response: "I'm not sure. I do know you don't have the bad habit of body shaming anymore!"

Hating my body was a horrible habit from which I have broken free. I hadn't worn shorts since high school, more than fifteen years ago. It wasn't because my body didn't fit into them, but because my heart was so overwhelmed with shame at wearing a size sixteen. On this date I had the shorts on, with a smile from ear to ear.

Keep going, Momma! I see you stepping up to the plate to overcome the struggle with weight loss and body shaming. You are doing a good work. We are pushing back darkness and breaking generational chains here.

ABOUT THE AUTHOR

Megan is living her dream life with her husband of 13 years and their 2 beautiful children. She is a homeschooling mom that also works outside the home as a Pediatric Physical Therapist. She has seen the scales staring back at her from 250 pounds all the way down to 150 pounds only to be looking at 230 pounds again. Megan is a trim healthy mama coach and a fitness teacher gospel preacher as a revelation wellness instructor. She empowers women to reclaim their life from the bondage of poor body image and the chains of an unhealthy relationship with food. She teaches simple strategies for food freedom starting with her free course dessert for breakfast.

You can grab her free course here: https://withmegandale.com/page/dessert-for-breakfast

23

THE TRUTH ABOUT SUCCESSFULLY
ADVOCATING FOR YOURSELF

DEBBIE DEAN

I had never thought about what it would mean to have a medically fragile child. I had never imagined a life of intravenous feeding, more medications than I could count, and the constant worry about whether my child would be okay or not. But that ended up becoming my reality.

During all my pregnancies I suffered from HG (hyperemesis gravidarum) which is an extreme form of nausea and vomiting. The first time it happened, I had no idea what was going on. From practically day one of that pregnancy, I was unable to keep anything down. When I simply couldn't take it anymore, I would ask my then husband to take me to the local emergency room. The only treatment they would offer were some IV fluids and nausea medication which would allow me to feel better for a few hours. I repeated that routine several times a week. I was uninsured, and sadly that was all the care the hospital would offer. Even the local OB doctor sent me a letter in the mail informing me they would not provide me with care due to my inability to pay. It didn't seem to matter that I was suffering from a potentially life-threatening condition for myself and my unborn child. I was experiencing extreme fatigue, lacking proper nourishment, and losing weight rapidly, yet no one would help.

I managed to survive each of my pregnancies, but there were some close calls. During the delivery of my son, my heart actually stopped. I remember whispering to the nurse that I was having a hard time breathing. It felt like someone was sitting on my chest, and then I passed out. I remember feeling like someone was hitting my chest really hard, and later I found out that the feeling was me being shocked by paddles in an attempt to get my heart started. Luckily, it worked—and I was saved. I was given a second chance to continue to be a mom to my kids. My baby was going to be okay. He was greatly underweight and needed to be in the NICU. But he was going to be fine, and so was I.

From birth, my daughter couldn't keep any nutrition down. She was unable to gain weight, and I had no idea what was wrong. I took her to her pediatrician nearly every week in an effort to get some answers, but her doctor would simply tell me that I was feeding her incorrectly. She told me to bring a bottle to the next appointment so that she could show me how to feed my daughter. At that appointment, the doctor witnessed my daughter projectile vomiting everywhere, as usual. She then recommended that she see a specialist and I promptly changed pediatricians. There was a several-months' waiting list to get in to see the specialist, and I felt so defeated. Fortunately, her new doctor had her admitted to the hospital. Here she was five months old already and barely getting the care she needed.

For years, that's how it went. Hospitalization after hospitalization. Doctor's visit upon doctor's visit. I was becoming bolder, asking more questions and demanding more answers. During one of her routine visits to her doctor, after a particularly high number of hospitalizations, he told me to take her home and pray for her. He didn't know if she would survive or not. Meanwhile, I was on IV nutrition carrying a risk of life-threatening infections. I had also begun to have kidney complications. I had to have a tube surgically placed in both my kidneys to help them function. Some days I didn't have the energy to care for myself, let alone my children. I would go without my IV nutrition because I was too ill to get out of bed and hook myself up to it. It was one of the most difficult times of my life.

Thankfully, the doctor was wrong that day, and my daughter survived. Still to this day, thirteen years later, she requires intravenous nutrition. Having her stomach constantly empty causes her to suffer from chronic heartburn. She had been on prescription medications for heartburn for several years, and I began to notice that slowly each medication was getting recalled. Others she had to stop taking due to the serious side effects they can cause with long term use. As a mom, this was a nightmare. I had to become my daughter's advocate overnight and research alternative ways to help support her body because the traditional ways were just not working. I found a plant-based supplement for her heartburn that she could take for as long as she needed, with no harmful side effects. I double checked it with her gastroenterologists, and they approved it for use. This was a game changer for us, and I finally felt empowered again at having a safe alternative to help her. She also has a surgically implanted feeding tube that brings many skin issues. I was able to find a safe cream for her to use without worrying about it causing her any other problems.

Throughout this journey, I had to let go of what others thought of my choices for her. There will always be others who don't agree with you, especially when it comes to our children, and they can get really loud about it. I knew that I knew her better than anyone else, though, and I trusted my experience as a nurse for over eighteen years. I learned to use my voice and no longer be afraid to talk about alternative ways of helping her with her doctors. I had no choice but to rise and empower myself as the advocate I wished I had had when I was so sick.

Being a single mom and having a child with chronic health issues is hard. It makes a regular nine-to-five job challenging. I don't get notice when my daughter is going to be sick and needs to be in the hospital. I have taken these difficult circumstances and through them have found a passion to help empower others to take more control over their health. Watching a person who has been struggling with health issues finally get relief and knowing they have someone they can turn to is amazing. I didn't have anyone to turn to back then, but I can be the person someone can turn to now.

I think it's important to demonstrate that Western medicine and alternative medicine can coexist. I firmly believe we should be treating our whole body. Not just physical symptoms but mental ones too because one can make the other one worse. It may take trial and error to find a provider who is willing to let you take more control, but it's worth it. We need to be our best advocates and find providers who respect our decisions.

I encourage you to seek other options, seek advice from providers who welcome alternative methods. You may be surprised at how many practitioners today are trained in alternative health. We don't have to suffer in silence anymore. There are so many people out there who have been through what you are going through. Let's help each other and encourage each other.

We need to end the stigma of risk attached to other ways besides what we are used to or what has been more mainstream. As one of my favorite health gurus says, "Gone are the days where the doctor knows everything, and the only treatment course is the one they prescribe." — Dr. Lindsey Elmore.

When we know better, we can do better. It's time to empower ourselves to be our best advocates because sometimes that's all we've got.

ABOUT THE AUTHOR

Debbie Dean has been a nurse by trade for over 18 years. She has 4 kids, ranging from 24 to 7 years old. Her daughter who was born with a chronic, life-threatening disease was her driving force to seek alternatives to traditional western medicine. She also experienced very traumatic pregnancies herself. For the first year of her daughters life, doctors didn't know if she would survive. Debbie started researching and learning more about alternative medicine. She was able to find alternatives to improve her daughters quality of life greatly. And make it possible for her daughter to stop using medicines that had very serious adverse side affects. Debbie saw a need to share this with others and started her business of Health Coaching.

Connect with her at dsdwholebodywellness.com

24

THE TRUTH ABOUT SUCCESSFULLY CULTIVATING PEACE DURING A SCARY DIAGNOSIS

CAROLYNN SAUER

My husband and I were sitting in the room at the high-risk pregnancy doctor's office, waiting for her to come in. We had four children already at home, but this was still a new experience for us. I am a planner (first born and female). I like to have a plan in mind, be in control (this is when God laughs) and have a backup plan to my backup plan. The longer we waited, the colder the room seemed to get, the harder the chairs felt, and the anxiety and stress grew by the minute.

The doctor told us there was good news, bad news, and potentially worse news. One of our baby's kidneys was very small and most likely non-functional. The good news was that most people's kidney function is around 80% when they have two. People can and have lived with one kidney, so while it's a concern, it's manageable. What the doctor was most concerned with was that there was also a spot on the baby's brain.

She explained that if the baby only had one of these issues, then they would just monitor my pregnancy very closely with lots of sonograms and bloodwork and classify this as a high-risk pregnancy. However, because the baby had a kidney issue and possibly a brain issue, they were very concerned. She went on to explain that technology gains were occurring so rapidly that they had no idea whether this was normal and they just hadn't ever seen it before, or if it really was an issue.

She mentioned that they were concerned about Trisomy 13 (I beg you NOT to google this, the pictures are graphic!) Basically, a baby with Trisomy 13 is born with an incomplete skull and "holes" in the face and head. Most babies don't ever make it home from the hospital. At that time, the longest a baby had lived with Trisomy 13 was six months. I'm pretty sure the doctor went on and gave us more information, but my mind had stopped listening. I suddenly felt the entire weight of the world on my shoulders, and I was stunned. After however long, I slowly started to become more present. The doctor recommended an amniocentesis and handed us a ton of brochures. She said that they could actually do the amnio that day, as the specialist was there and had an opening. "I'll let you two have some time to process, discuss and come up with questions," the doctor said as she made her way out of the room.

Still stunned and feeling super heavy, I stared into space for a while. I knew that there were major risks to an amniocentesis, and that was terrifying. Eventually, I asked my husband what he was thinking. He, of course, had been frantically looking stuff up on his phone. He said that especially since we already had four kids at home, and considering how much of a planner I am, he thought we should have the amniocentesis performed. His reasoning was that if we didn't, I would stress so much about it that the stress could be detrimental to me and the baby. Not to mention that if we were having a baby with such a severe and life-threatening disability, we'd need to prepare our other children for the possibility of a baby that would more than likely never come home; or, if the baby did miraculously make it out of the hospital, what the short time at home might look like. While feeling like I was having an out-of-body experience, I understood his logic and marveled at and was utterly grateful for the fact that he could think so clearly at a time like this.

The doctor came back into the room and my first question was, "If we do the amniocentesis and our baby has something life threatening, how much pressure will we be put under to have an abortion?" She told us that her job was to present facts, statistics, professional experiences and choices, but that the decisions were always ultimately ours. After going over the potential risks and complications again, we made the decision to go ahead and get the amniocentesis, and to do it that day.

As we waited for them to prepare the procedure room, it took every ounce of energy for me to stay in the chair. All I wanted to do was run home to the babies I already had, to hug them, to look into their eyes and tell them how much I loved them, to remember how much of a miracle they were and just be overly grateful for the blessing of them. The blessing of motherhood. The blessing of the hard days. The blessing of love and the unconditional love I had for them, simply because they were mine.

We were called back to the procedure room, and they got me prepped and everything ready. The doctor explained the procedure, and every little thing to expect in detail. She said to expect a lot of pressure. They did a sonogram to figure out the location and positioning of the baby, and to determine the best place from which to draw out the amniotic fluid. Iodine was applied to the injection site and she pushed the extraction needle into my abdomen. I felt like there had been a 100-pound weight thrust around in my belly, trying to get out. I yelled, "Ouch!" and then immediately apologized and said, "I have no idea why I yelled that, it didn't hurt at all, it just utterly surprised me."

The immense feeling of the pressure redistribution was astonishing, and words completely fail to describe the sensation. The nurse cleaned off my belly and put a Band-Aid over the injection site. The contrast between such a small, ordinary item

—an adhesive strip I've used numerous times to comfort and care for my children—and the immensity of the procedure, test results, and possible future seemed like an irony.

By this point I was exhausted. I knew I needed sleep and food but was so tired I couldn't even fathom which one I needed more. I was shocked at how much this whole experience had taken out of me. I thought I'd known what tired was. Anyone who has had a newborn knows and completely understands how sleep deprivation is a form of torture, but this was a whole new level for me.

One week.

Test results would be back in a week. That was one of the longest weeks of my life. I remember loving and hugging my family, thanking God, and just appreciating every single aspect of being a mom during that week. I tried not to think about what the future might hold, but when you know you're not supposed to do something, human nature kicks in: We usually go ahead and do it anyway. I thought a lot about the words that an acquaintance who had a child with many health issues had said to me many years before. She needed someone to watch her youngest so that she could go to the hospital to be with her sick child for a few hours. I volunteered to help, and when she dropped off her child, I happened to mention that I didn't know how she did it all. She spun around so fast and said, "I hate it when people say that to me, because I know you cannot stand there and tell me that if this were your child that you wouldn't be doing the exact same things as I am." I was taken aback and speechless, but she was right. If that were my child (if that were a glimpse of what our future might look like), I knew we would do everything we had to do.

The phone rang, I picked it up and heard, "Hi, is this Carolynn? I'm ___ from Dr. ___'s office and I'm calling about your test results. I'm happy to report that the amniocentesis indicates you have a genetically perfectly healthy baby boy!"

(Insert automatic ugly cry; tears streaming down my face.) I hung up the phone, wrapped my arms around my belly and said a thanksgiving prayer to God for yet another blessing upon blessing. For the rest of the pregnancy, I was cloaked in gratitude.

That sweet little boy is now in first grade and makes us laugh every single day. He ended up being born with two kidneys, but one was tiny and non-functioning, so his body eventually absorbed it (completely expected). For the first two years of his life, he had to have blood work and a sonogram every six months. Now he only has to do that once a year. We have to make sure he doesn't get dehydrated, but his one kidney is functioning at a higher-than-normal percentage (yay!). The specialist has said that issues may start arising as he gets older, as his body gets bigger and requires more work from the kidney. For now, we are grateful for everyday there is no problem and are slowly teaching him lifestyle habits to support his kidney. We are blessed.

ABOUT THE AUTHOR

Carolynn Sauer is a wife and mom to six. She has four boys and two girls ranging from ages fifteen to three and they live in Wichita, Kansas. Carolynn comes from a long line of teachers and her mother did home day care for thirteen years of her childhood. She had her first paid babysitting job at the age of eight. Carolynn babysat all the time, was a nanny, taught swimming lessons, worked in multiple day care centers and has a degree in Elementary Education and Early Childhood. She taught for five years and then became a stay at home mom. Carolynn is currently a stay at home mom (or personal driver), life coach and a Barre instructor.

Connect with her at MyLittleBitofLife.com

25

THE TRUTH ABOUT SUCCESSFULLY OVERCOMING THE BULLY WITHIN

FAYE HARTZELL

Two-zero-zero-point-three. Two hundred point three. 200.3. I looked, got off and on twice, and after grasping the reality of it wondered: *How did I get here?* The only time the scale had ever displayed a number like that, I was nine months pregnant. At least I had gotten a baby out of that deal. This, this was purely the result of a tormented heart and chocolate-chip cookies.

Ashamed, defeated and feeling literally suffocated at times, I was miserable on the inside. Every so often, when my mind would not allow me to escape its thoughts, I would release the breath I didn't even realize I had been holding. Like flood waters weaving their way, progressively reaching every crevice before creeping onward, so shame takes hold, choking all in its path, including the life its victim was meant to live.

This moment, this two-hundred-point-three moment, was just waiting to be defined. Its definition could remain, as it had for years, another reminder of failure; or maybe, just maybe, it could be rewritten. At that moment, standing on that scale, a new definition began to be engraved on my heart. Unlike entering a word into a search engine and instantly receiving its meaning, pronunciation, and application, mine was not an instant definition. It began with God whispering, "I love you," followed by revealing the secrets and lies, and learning how to live an authentic life. It was not an instant definition; but day by day He would teach me to apply it, as I believed Him.

Obviously, I needed to do something different. I didn't need baby steps. I needed a radical—something I had never done nor believed I could do—kind of step. Then, as I scrolled through the happenings of the day on Facebook, there it was: a post advertising a local run, a half marathon! I'd participated in a few 5K races in the past, but nothing more. I looked at the post and thought, *"That would be a challenge."* I clicked the link, filled out the form, entered my credit card information and pressed "submit" before I could talk myself out of it. I felt a knot begin to form in the pit of my stomach when I received the confirmation email that I was officially signed up.

I chose to participate in walk/run training, as having extra weight was hard enough. Putting an unreasonable amount of pressure on myself to run the entire thing was something I was unwilling to do. I wanted to finish *alive*. You may think I'm being dramatic, but you must realize that I had never committed to anything wellness-related for more than a few weeks. This would most definitely be a challenge on every level. Physically, emotionally, and spiritually.

Not just any run, either. I decided to call this my "Freedom Run." I was making a choice to rid myself of the negative emotions bottled up in my mind and hurting my heart. The run represented deliverance from all the thoughts holding me back, the lies I believed about myself, the pain, the disappointment of unrealized expectations and every other thing hindering my ability to dream "big" and to follow those dreams.

It was time.

"Seriously, you think you're going to finish the race? You missed two runs last week."

"Everyone will be looking at you. You don't look like a runner. You know they'll be laughing at you."

"You're never going to finish."

"ENOUGH!" I yelled.

Yelling made no difference, as no one heard me. Those comments weren't being spoken to me, they were coming from me, inside my head.

There has been so much talk about bullying and the importance of teaching our children not to do it. Yet some of us, probably more than we are willing to admit, bully on a regular basis; we bully ourselves. Every time we don't start something because we are unsure we can do it, every time we don't do something we really want to do because of what we're afraid others will think, every time we look in a mirror and think negative thoughts—every one of these times and every other time we hold ourselves back, we are a bully. Maybe the most harmful bully of all, because we are in this bully's presence every moment of every day.

What would you tell your friends dealing with a bully who never left them alone? What if that bully was verbally abusing them every waking moment of the day? What if your friends told you their dreams are interrupted by this bully?

There's a good chance you would urge them to get help from someone and to stand up to the bully, and you would do whatever it took to get the bullies to stop, wouldn't you? Well, guess what? That is exactly what you have to do with the bully within. It may be hard, but trust me, it's possible.

It begins with the simple act of making a list. I listed the negative thoughts I had about myself and evaluated each to see if it was true. If it wasn't, I simply refused to allow myself to think it anymore. If it was something that I had believed for a long time and it crept in, I immediately thought of something I know to be positive about who I am. It's all about intentional thinking and changing the thoughts and the lies we've allowed define us.

If the negative thing was true, I then had a choice to make. Did it bother me enough to make me change my behavior and not have it be a part of my life anymore, or was I okay with it? It really is that simple. If I don't like something about myself, only I have the ability to change it. I can't change it by complaining about it, making excuses for it, or ignoring it. I can only change it by *doing* something about it. It's not easy, but it can be done. If I'm not willing to change it, I have to stop complaining about it.

I knew I wasn't going to be able to change some of these behaviors quickly or without help, so I enlisted some friends to help me. They became not only my cheerleaders but also helped me remain accountable for the new habits I was trying to form.

The hardest part was being totally honest with them about what I was struggling with. Who wants to admit they've only been exercising once or twice a week when they really need to be exercising four or five? Who wants to admit that they have a love affair with carbs and need to make better food choices? Who wants to say they can't have certain snack food in the house because they don't have the willpower not to eat it? What I realized was that I didn't *want* to say these things, but I *needed* to say them because I wasn't at a point I could do it on my own yet. I needed help. There is nothing wrong with recognizing when you need help and reaching out to others. I needed someone to talk to when I began slipping back into old habits. Most of the time I was able to recognize if I was dwelling on a bad thought and could snap myself out of it by praying, listening to uplifting music or deliberately getting involved in something to take my mind off of that thing.

Doing these things on a daily basis is what changed the negative continuous loop that had been running in my head for decades. Recognizing I had the ability to change the loop that governs my thoughts and ultimately my actions is what changed my entire life. It's what allowed me to run across that finish line and wear that finisher's medal proudly. It's now my life's mission to help others do the same.

Finding the truth about who you were created to be and using that truth to serve others: it's in that, and only that, you find true success.

ABOUT THE AUTHOR

Faye Hartzell is an Author, Speaker, Professional Life Coach & AFT Practitioner.

For many years the pain of the past was like an invisible chain, the links of that chain being reminders of childhood trauma. Those links, bound so tightly together, would allow her to be an active participant in daily life but kept her tethered to a wall of shame. She has spent years unpacking the baggage of that shame.

It's now her passion to share with as many women as she can, the blueprint to releasing the pain of the past and what's holding them back to create a joy-filled, purpose-driven future.

Connect with Faye here: www.fayehartzell.com

ACKNOWLEDGMENTS

What an amazing journey this has been! First and foremost I want to thank Jesus for bringing this collaboration to life. He is my everything. Thank you to my fellow authors for jumping in and saying YES! To Martha Krejci I will likely thank you in every book I write because you have impacted my life so profoundly and I would not be who I am today without you. To my incredibly husband and kids thank you for giving me grace through a project we didn't realize would be so time consuming. I love you more than words can say. Cee, you are my favourite editor on the planet, thank you for everything. And finally, thank YOU dear reader for grabbing this book and supporting twenty-five authors who are changing the world.

xo Meggan

Made in the USA
Coppell, TX
26 August 2021